# A
# GUIDE TO TAXILA

# A GUIDE TO TAXILA

BY

**SIR JOHN MARSHALL**, KT., C.I.E., M.A.,
Litt.D., F.S.A., Hon. A.R.I.B.A., ETC.,
director General of Archaeology in India

GYAN

*Published by*

GYAN

Gyan Publishing House
5, Ansari Road
Daryaganj, New Delhi-110002
Phone: 011-47034999, 9811692060
E-mail: books@gyanbooks.com

*Distribution Network*
gyanbooks.com
India, USA, Canada, UK, Australia, France



ISBN : 978-81-212-2418-5 (HB)
First Published, 1918

2nd Impression 2021

*Printed at:* Gyan Press, Delhi.



**A**
**Guide to Taxila**
Author: Sir John Marshall

# A GUIDE TO TAXILA

BY

SIR JOHN MARSHALL, KT., C.I.E., M.A.,

Litt.D., F.S.A., Hon.A.R.I.B.A., ETC.,

Director General of Archæology in India

CALCUTTA

SUPERINTENDENT GOVERNMENT PRINTING, INDIA

1918

PLATE I.

HEAD OF DIONYSUS, SIRKAP.

Photo-engraved & printed at the Offices of the Survey of India, Calcutta, 1918.

# CONTENTS

# LIST OF PLATES

# A GUIDE TO TAXILA

## CHAPTER I

### Topography

LOCATION OF TAXILA AND CHARACTER OF COUNTRY IN ANCIENT TIMES.

The remains of Taxila are situated immediately to the east and north-east of Sarai-kala, a junction on the railway, twenty miles north-west of Rawalpindi.[1] The valley in which they lie is a singularly pleasant one, well-watered by the Haro river and its tributaries, and protected by a girdle of hills—on the north and east by the snow mountains of Hazara and the Murree ridge, on the south and west by the well-known Margalla spur and other lower eminences. This position on the great trade route, which used to connect Hindustan with Central and Western Asia, coupled

[1] There are good refreshment and waiting rooms for travellers at Sarai-kala railway station, and a small Public Works' bungalow about a mile distant, permission to occupy which may sometimes be obtained from the Executive Engineer, Rawalpindi District. Less than half a mile from the station is the Archæological Office, where information can be obtained regarding the excavations. The building of the local museum, which is contemplated for Taxila, has had to be postponed for the present, but by the courtesy of the Director General visitors are allowed, during the time that excavations are actually in progress, to see the antiquities in the storerooms at the Archæological Bungalow. Excavations are carried on only in the autumn and spring.

with the strength of its natural defences, the fertility of its soil, and a constant supply of good water, readily account for the importance of the city in early times. Arrian speaks of it as being a great and flourishing city in the time of Alexander the Great, the greatest, indeed, of all the cities which lay between the Indus and the Hydaspes (Jihlam).[1] Strabo tells us that the country round about was thickly populated, and extremely fertile, as the mountains here begin to subside into the plains,[2] and Plutarch[3] remarks on the richness of the soil. Hsüan Tsang,[4] also, writes in a similar strain of the land's fertility, of its rich harvests, of its flowing streams and of its luxuriant vegetation.

From the map on Plate XXIX it will be seen that stretching across this tract of country, from north-east by east to south-west by west, is a ridge of hills of which the western termination is called Hathiāl. This ridge of hills is a rocky and precipitous spur of limestone formation, which projects into the valley from the mountains on the East, and divides the eastern part of it into two halves. The northern half is now-a-days singularly rich in crops, being watered by numerous artificial canals taken off from the higher reaches of the Haro river; the southern half is less fertile, being intersected by many deep ravines and broken by bare stony knolls, on many of which are ruins of old-time stūpas and monasteries. Through

[1] Bk. V, Ch. 3. *Cf.* McCrindle, *The invasion of India by Alexander the Great*, p. 92.
[2] Bk. XV, Ch. 28. McCrindle, *Ancient India*, p. 33.
[3] Ch. LIX.
[4] Watters, *On Yuan Chwang*, Vol. I, p. 240.

this part of the valley and skirting the western foot of the Hathiāl hill runs the Tabra or Tamrā nālā, which is manifestly identical with the stream called Tiberonabo, Tiberoboam, or Tiberio-potamos referred to by classical authors.[1] Through the northern half of the valley flows the Luṇḍī nālā, another tributary of the Haro river, which like the Tamrā nālā now runs in a deep bed, but in old days, no doubt, was nearer the surface.

**BHIṚ MOUND.**

Within this valley and within three and a half miles of each other are the remains of three distinct cities. The southernmost of these occupies an elevated plateau, known locally as the Bhiṛ mound, between the recently opened railway from Sarai-kala to Havelian and the Tamrā nālā, above the bed of which it rises to a height of between 60 and 70 feet. From north to south this plateau measures about 1,210 yards and from east to west, at its widest point, about 730. On its western and southern sides its boundaries follow a fairly regular line, but on the east and north they sweep along the edges of the bays and bluffs above the Tamrā nālā, and in some of these bays, where the soil has been washed down into the ravine below, it is no longer possible to trace with accuracy the original position of the walls. According to local tradition, the Bhiṛ mound is the most ancient of all the sites at Taxila, and this tradition is fully confirmed by the discoveries which I have made on the surface of the mound. Gen. Cunningham was of opinion that this city was still in occupation at the

[1] *Cf.* Sylvain Levi, *J. A.*, Tome XV (8me Serie), pp. 236-7, and McCrindle, *Ancient India*, pp. 342-3.

time of Hsüan Tsang's visit in the 7th century A.D., but this opinion appears to have rested on no surer ground than his own speculations as to the identity of a ruined stūpa in the region of Babarkhāna with the stūpa of the 'Head gift' described by the Chinese pilgrim, which, as we shall presently see, has proved to be erroneous. It is certainly not borne out by existing remains, which indicate that the Bhiṛ mound was occupied as a city many centuries prior to the coming of the Greeks, and that the capital was transferred by them in the early part of the 2nd century B.C. to the area now known as Sirkap.

SIRKAP. This second city of Sirkap, of which almost the entire outer wall is still clearly visible, occupies the western spurs of the hill of Hathiāl, together with a well-defined plateau on their northern side. On the western edge of this plateau the city wall has an irregular alignment broken by various salients and recesses, but on the north and east it is quite straight, and from the south-east corner of the plateau it proceeds in the same straight line up the steep side of the northern ridge of Hathiāl, then drops across a valley, traverses a second ridge and depression, and so ascends to the summit of the third and highest ridge on the south. From this point it turns in a westerly direction and descends the rocky edge of the ridge to its western corner; after which it takes a sharp turn to the north, and bends west again around a prominent bluff above the Tamrā nālā, and so returns north along the western face of the plateau. Within its circuit the city wall thus takes in three rocky and precipitous ridges of the Hathiāl spur, besides an isolated flat-topped hill, which rises in a gradual slope from the bluff above referred to, and the whole of the level plateau to their north. The length of this wall is approximately 6,000 yards, its thickness varying from 15 ft. to 21 ft. 6 in. Throughout its whole length both the core and facing of the wall are composed of rubble stones of no great size or stability, the construction being in all respects similar to that of other structures of the Greek and Śaka-Pahlava epochs, and, like them, liable to fall rapidly to ruin. The outer curtain of the wall is strengthened by bastions which, so far as they have been examined, are rectangular in plan (p. 65).

To judge by its position and configuration, it seems probable that the isolated flat-topped hill mentioned above was the real Akropolis of the ancient city of Sirkap; but it is likely that the whole of the area comprised within the Hathiāl ridges and between them and this hill was also specially fortified to serve as a place of refuge in case of siege. To this end an inner line of fortifications appears to have been carried along the north side of the Akropolis, as well as along the base of the northern ridge of Hathiāl, the only access to the interior fort being provided by a gateway in the depression between the two hills. Gen. Cunningham imagined that this gateway was directly opposite to the northern gate of the city and connected with it by a straight street leading through the middle of the lower city, but excavations in this part of the site show that his ideas on this point were incorrect.

BABAR KHĀNA OR KACHCHĀ KOṬ.

Outside the northern wall of the Sirkap city was a suburb, now known as Babar-khāna or the Kachchā Koṭ from the fact that it is defended by earthen ramparts only. This suburb has a circuit of rather more than a mile and a quarter, and is enclosed on the west in a bend of the Tamrā nālā, above which its fortifications rise to a height of about 40 feet.

SIRSUKH.

The third city is that of Sirsukh, situated still further to the north-east, on the opposite side of the Luṇḍī nālā. This city appears to have been built by the Kushāns, probably during the reign of Kanishka. Its plan is roughly a parallelogram, and the circuit of the walls is not far short of three miles. The walls, which are relatively well-preserved along part of the southern and eastern sides, are of massive construction, some 18 feet or more in thickness and protected by circular bastions on their outer side. The facing of the walls is of the 'large diaper' masonry which came into vogue in the early Kushān period; the bastions are circular,[1] and the intervals between them measure 90 feet. Inside the city are three modern villages, Mīrpur, Tofkiāñ, and Piṇḍ Gākhṛā, placed on the remains of ancient buildings, which are still peeping out from the débris among the houses.

MONUMENTS OUTSIDE THE CITIES.

In addition to these three city sites—the Bhiṛ mound, Sirkap and Sirsukh—there are many other detached monuments, mainly Buddhist stūpas and monasteries, scattered about over the face of the surrounding country. The Buddhist remains are specially numerous in the southern half of the valley, where they occupy most of the barren hillocks alongside the Tamrā nālā, conspicuous among them being the imposing Dharmarājikā Stūpa, known locally as the

[1] Not square, as shown by Gen. Cunningham.

"Chir" or "Split" Tope, from the great cleft which former explorers drove through its centre. In the northern half of the valley, however, and among the hills of the Hathiāl ridge are many other Buddhist settlements, of which five have already been excavated and have yielded results of surpassing interest. These are the Kunāla Stūpa and monastery which stand on the northern ridge of Hathiāl, partly covering the old city wall of Sirkap; the stūpas and monasteries at Mohṛā Morādu and Jauliāñ in the same range of hills further to the east; and those at Bādalpur and Lālchak in the valley to the north. At Jaṇḍiāl, a little to the north of the Kachchā Koṭ, are two conspicuous mounds, on one of which is a spacious temple, dedicated, there is good reason to believe, to fire-worship; and a little beyond these, again, are the remains of two smaller stūpas—which may have been either Jaina or Buddhist, probably the former. Still further north a conspicuous land-mark is furnished by the lofty Bhallaṛ Stūpa, which occupies a prominent position on the last spur of the hills bounding the valley of Taxila on the north. Beside these remains there are, dotted here and there in the valleys and hills, many other eminences of ancient days, but the sites mentioned above are the only ones that have yet been excavated, and it is unnecessary here to enter into particulars regarding the others.

## CHAPTER II

### HISTORY

Notwithstanding the power and wealth of Taxila in ancient days, the information we possess regarding its history is singularly meagre, being drawn in the main from the accounts of Greek or Chinese writers, or laboriously pieced together with the help of coins and a few rare inscriptions. The name of the city was Takkasilā or Takhaśilā (in Sanskrit Takshaśilā),[1] which in Greek and Roman writers was transcribed as Taxila. The foundation of the earliest city goes back to a very remote age. In the Mahābhārata[2] it is mentioned in connexion with the great snake sacrifice of King Janamejaya, by whom it had been conquered. Later on—about the beginning, that is to say, of the 5th century before our era—it was probably included in the Achæmenid Empire of Persia; for the inscriptions of Darius at Persepolis and on his tomb at Naksh-i-Rustam make mention of a new Indian satrapy, which was regarded as the richest and most populous in the Empire and which, being distinct

PERSIAN EMPIRE.

[1] Meaning probably "The city of cut stone."

[2] The more important references to Taxila in Indian literature have been collected by Dr. V. S. Sukthankar. *A. S. R.*, 1914-15, Pt. II, pp. 36-41.

from Aria, Arachosia and Gandaria, may be assumed to have comprised Sind and a considerable part of the Panjab east of the Indus.[1] An interesting relic of Persian influence at Taxila is an inscription in Aramaic characters of the 4th or 5th century B.C., the only Aramaic record that has yet been found in India (p. 75). That Taxila at this time and during the centuries immediately following enjoyed a great reputation as a University town, famous for the arts and sciences of the day, is evident from numerous passages in the Buddhist Jātakas; but, apart from this fact, virtually nothing is known of its history prior to the invasion of Alexander the Great. That monarch descended on the Panjab and received the submission of Taxila in the spring of 326 B.C., halting there for some weeks preparatory to his attack on Porus. From the extant accounts of Alexander's expedition, based on the writings of his own companions or contemporaries, we learn that the city was then very wealthy, populous and well governed, and that its territories extended from the Indus to the Hydaspes. We learn, too, that polygamy and the practice of *satī* were in vogue; that girls too poor to be wedded were exposed for sale in the market place; and that the bodies of the dead were thrown to the vultures. At the time of Alexander's invasion, the reigning king Āmbhi, known to the Greeks as Omphis or Taxiles,[2] was at war not only with the

ALEXANDER THE GREAT.

[1] *Cf.* V. S. Smith, *Early History of India*, 3rd Ed., p. 38. On the other hand, some of the Jātakas refer to Taxila as a capital city of Gandhāra itself.

[2] Manifestly a territorial title.

powerful kingdom of Porus, on the further side of the Jihlam, but with the neighbouring Hill State of Abhisāra, and it was no doubt in the hope of securing Alexander's help against these foes that he sent an embassy to wait upon the Macedonian at Und (Udabhāṇḍa) and led out his troops in person from Taxila, in order to place them at the service of the conqueror, afterwards entertaining him with lavish hospitality at the capital and providing a contingent of five thousand men for the expedition against Porus. In return for these and other friendly acts Āmbhi was confirmed in the possession of his own territories and rewarded by the accession of new ones, while his position was further strengthened by a reconciliation with Porus.

The Macedonian conquest of North-Western India was a splendid achievement; but its effects were short-lived. Alexander had intended the permanent annexation of the North-West, and for that purpose he left colonies and garrisons behind him to consolidate what he had won, but within six years of his death, which took place in 323 B.C., Eudemus, the Greek Governor, withdrew from the Indus valley with all the forces he could muster to assist Eumenes against Antiochus, and about the same time, or perhaps even earlier, Chandragupta drove out the Greek garrisons east of the Indus, and proceeded to incorporate Taxila and the other states of the Panjab into the Empire of Magadha. Then followed, about 305 B.C., the

**Seleucus Nicātōr.**

transient and ineffective invasion of Seleucus Nicātōr, who sought to reconquer the lost possessions of Alexander, but was reduced to making a hasty and humiliating peace with Chandragupta, under the terms of which all the old Macedonian provinces, as far as the Hindu Kush, were ceded to the Indian Monarch.[1] To the states of the Panjab the iron hand of Chandragupta must have proved more oppressive than that of the Greeks before him, and, when his son Bindusāra succeeded to the throne of Magadha, Taxila threw off the Maurya yoke and was not, seemingly, brought to submission until the Crown prince Aśoka himself appeared before its gates. Aśoka afterwards ruled here as Viceroy on behalf of Bindusāra, and during his father's and his own life-time he appears to have maintained the Maurya power throughout the North-West no less efficiently, though perhaps less harshly, than did his grandfather Chandragupta. To him, no doubt, was subsequently due much of the strength which Buddhism gained in this part of India.[2]

MAURYA EMPIRE.

Soon after Aśoka's death, which occurred about the year 231 B.C., the empire of Magadha began to break up, and Taxila, along with other outlying provinces, was able once again to assert her independence, only to fall an easy prey to fresh Greek invaders from Bactria, whom the decline of the Maurya power invited eastward. These invaders were the descendants of

BACTRIAN GREEKS.

[1] The hasty conclusion of this peace, by which Seleucus Nicātōr received only 500 elephants in exchange for so vast a tract of country was probably due no less to the danger with which he was threatened by Antigonus in the West, than to the unexpectedly strong opposition of Chandragupta, though Seleucus must have recognised the impracticability of ever effectively holding the disputed provinces.

[2] There is a tradition recorded by Hsüan Tsang to the effect that Khotan was first colonized by exiles from Taxila, banished by Aśoka after the blinding of his son, Kunāla. See pp. 60-61 *infra*, and Stein, *Ancient Khotan*, I, pp. 156 sqq.

the Greek colonies which Alexander the Great had planted in Bactria and which, unlike the colonies of the Panjab, had taken firm root and flourished. Thus, although the Macedonian's conquest of the Panjab made no permanent impression upon India, his conquest of the neighbouring countries was indirectly responsible for the subsequent establishment of Greek culture and Greek art in the north-west. The first of the Bactrian invaders to reach Taxila was Demetrius, son-in-law of Antiochus the Great (c. 190 B.C.), who carried his arms successfully through the Kābul valley, the Panjab and Sind. Twenty years later came Eucratides, who wrested first Bactria and then part of his Indian possessions, including Taxila, from Demetrius. From these two conquerors there sprang two rival lines of princes, who continued in India the feud which had been started in Bactria,[1] encroaching from time to time upon each other's territories. Among the Greek kings who ruled over Taxila, Apollodotus and Menander apparently belonged to the house of Demetrius, Antialcidas to that of Eucratides.[2] Of the many other Greek rulers in the Panjab and North-West our knowledge at present is too meagre to determine which of them ruled at Taxila, and what connexion, if any, they had with the one or the other of these two houses.

SCYTHIANS AND PARTHIANS.

The rule of the Greeks at Taxila had endured for little more than a century, when it was swept away

[1] *Cf.* Rapson, *Ancient India*, p. 128.

[2] *Op. cit.*, p. 133. Other authorities take Apollodotus to be a son of Eucratides. Cunningham, *Numismatic Chron.*, 1869, pp. 241-3.

by invading hosts of barbarians from the west. These barbarians were the Scythians or Śakas, as they were known in India, who had long been settled in the Parthian Province of Seistan, and had there mingled and intermarried freely with the Parthian elements in the population. From Seistan they overran Arachosia and the neighbouring countries, and thence passed across the Indus to the conquest of the Panjab. In Arachosia one section of these invaders remained and established its supremacy under the leadership of a Parthian named Vonones; while another section, under the Śaka chief Maues, pressed eastward and conquered the kingdom of Taxila. Maues appears to have risen to power in Arachosia about 95 B.C., and to have reached Taxila some ten or fifteen years later. He was succeeded in or about 58 B.C. by Azes I, who had been intimately associated with the family of Vonones in the Government of Arachosia, and was, in fact, perhaps as much a Parthian as a Śaka. Though little is known of Azes I, there can be no doubt that his reign was a long and prosperous one, and it is probable that he was responsible for extending and consolidating the Śaka power throughout North-West India as far as the banks of the Jumna. In the administration of his dominions he adopted the old Persian system of government by Satraps, which had long been established in the Panjab, and this same system was continued by his successors, Azilises and Azes II, whose local satraps at Taxila and Mathura[1] were also of the Śaka race and connected with one another by close family ties.

[1] Liaka-Kusulaka, Pātika, Rājūvula, and Śoḍāsa.

On the death of Azes II, the kingdoms of Taxila and Arachosia were united under one rule by the Parthian Gondopharnes, the fame of whose power spread to the Western world, and who figured in early Christian writings as the prince to whose court St. Thomas the Apostle was sent. This union of the two kingdoms took place about the third decade of our era and may be presumed to have been a peaceful one. After its achievement Gondopharnes proceeded to annex the Kābul valley, overthrowing the Greek principality in that region and driving out the last prince Hermaeus. But there could have been little cohesion in this empire of Gondopharnes; for no sooner had his personal authority been removed than the satraps of the various Provinces asserted their own sovereignty. Abdagases, the nephew of Gondopharnes, took the Western Panjab; Orthagnes, and after him Pakores, Arachosia and Sind; and other parts of his dominions fell to other princelings, among whom were Sasan, Sapedanes, and Satavastra, whose coins I have discovered for the first time at Taxila.

**Apollonius of Tyāna.** It was during the Indo-Parthian supremacy, probably in the year 44 A.D., that Apollonius of Tyāna is reputed to have visited Taxila. According to his biographer Philostratus, the king then reigning at Taxila was named Phraotes, who was independent of Vardanes, the Parthian king of Babylon, and himself powerful enough to exercise suzerain power over the satrapy of Gandhāra.[1] Approaching Taxila from

[1] It is worthy of remark that Phraotes found it necessary to pay subsidies to the wilder tribes on his frontier in order to keep them quiet.

the north-west, Apollonius halted at a temple in front of the wall, which he describes in some detail, and which, as we shall presently see, may possibly be identical with the temple at Jaṇḍiāl. The city itself, *viz.*, the city of Sirkap, was, he says, about the same size as Nineveh and fortified like the cities of Greece on a symmetrical plan.[1] The streets were narrow and irregular like the streets of Athens, and the houses had the appearance of being one-storied, but had in reality basement rooms underground. Inside the city was a temple of the Sun and a royal palace, the latter of which was distinguished by its simplicity and lack of ostentation, very different from the splendour which Philostratus had seen at the court of Babylon.

The credibility of the story of Apollonius as related by Philostratus has been reasonably questioned by modern critics, and there is no doubt that there is much fiction in it mingled with the truth. On the other hand, there is little in the account of Taxila which is not borne out by what we know of the history of those times, while some details find remarkably strong corroboration in my own discoveries. It is a reasonable inference, therefore, that Apollonius did in fact journey as far as Taxila, and that Philostratus had access to the notes of his companion Damis. These notes were probably correct so far as his own personal observations went, but coloured by hearsay stories related to him ; and it is likely that other " travellers'

[1] The words τετειχίσθαι δὲ ξυμμέτρως are translated by Conybeare " fairly well fortified," but this can hardly be the meaning here

tales". were culled by Apollonius from earlier Greek writers, in order to enliven his narrative.

**Hermæus and the Kushāns.** To revert, however, to the history of Taxila. The opportunity of recovering his lost kingdom which the dismemberment of the Indo-Parthian Empire offered to Hermæus was not lost upon him. After being driven from Kābul, he appears to have formed an alliance with Kujūla Kadphises, the powerful chief of the Kushāns, and with his help to have won back Kābul, and afterwards to have combined with him in the conquest of Gandhāra and Taxila.[1] These Kushāns were a tribe of the people called by the Chinese historians Yüeh-chih,[2] who emanated originally from the extreme north-west of China. From China they were driven westward about 170 B.C., and proceeded to occupy, first, Bactria and the region of the Oxus valley; then the Kābul valley; and, finally, the plains of Northern India. The chronology of this period is very uncertain, but it seems probable that it was about 50 or 60 A.D. that Kujūla Kadphises and Hermæus wrested the Kābul valley and Taxila from the Parthians, and a few years later that Kujūla was succeeded by Wima Kadphises, who consolidated and enlarged the empire which his predecessor had won. To about this period belong the coins of the nameless ruler commonly known as Soter Megas, who may have been a successor of Wima Kadphises.[3] Then followed, in the second century

[1] See p. 9 *ante*, footnote 1.

[2] The Yüeh-chih are commonly known as the Kushāns, because it was to the particular Kushān tribe that their kings belonged.

[3] There seems to me to have been a break between the reigns of Kadphises II and Kanishka.

of our era, the great and powerful Kanishka, the most famous of all the Kushāns, and after him Huvishka and Vāsudeva. Kanishka made his winter capital at Purushapura, the modern Peshawar, and extended his conquests over a wide area, from Central Asia to the borders of Bengal, and it is probable that this empire was maintained intact by his immediate successors. The death of Vāsudeva probably occurred in the first half of the third century A.D., and from this time forward the Kushān power gradually declined,[1] though it survived in the Panjab until the invasion of the White Huns or Ephthalites in the 5th century of our era.

In the year 400 A.D. the Chinese pilgrim Fa Hien visited the Buddhist monuments at Taxila, but unfortunately has left us no particulars about them. From his accounts of other places in that part of India however, it is evident that at the time of his pilgrimage the great Buddhist sanctuaries of the North-West were still relatively vigorous and flourishing; and it is no less evident from the condition in which they have been unearthed, that the monuments of Taxila were wantonly and ruthlessly devastated in the course of the same century. This work of destruction is almost certainly to be attributed to the hordes of barbarian White Huns, who after the year 455 A.D. swept down into India in ever increasing numbers, carrying sword and fire wherever they went, and not only possessed themselves of the kingdom of the Kushāns, but

DESTRUCTION BY THE WHITE HUNS.

[1] The decline of the Kushān power may have been hastened by an unrecorded Sasanian invasion. Many Sasanian coins have been unearthed at Taxila.

eventually overthrew the great Empire of the Guptas.

HŪSAN TSANG. From this calamity Taxila never again recovered, and when Hsüan Tsang visited it in the seventh century, he found it had become a dependency of Kashmir, that the local chiefs were at feud with one another, and that most of the monasteries were ruined and desolate.[1]

MODERN EXPLORATIONS. Of the exploration of the remains at Taxila up to the time when the writer started his operations, there is little to chronicle. Like most ancient sites in this part of India, it was long subjected to the depredations of amateur archæologists or treasure-seekers. Among the former were Major Pearse, Major Cracroft, Deputy Commissioner of Rawalpindi, and Mr. Delmerick. Of the latter one of the worst offenders was a *bhisti* of the village of S̲h̲āh Ḍherī named Nur, who in the fifties and sixties of last century seems to have made his living by opening small stūpas in the neighbourhood and disposing of their contents to Government officials or antiquity dealers. He it was who discovered an inscribed gold plate in one of the stūpas near Jaṇḍiāl and despoiled many other structures of their relics. It was not, however, until 1863, when Gen. Cunningham turned his attention to the site, that its identity with the ancient Taxila was established. This identity, which Gen. Cunningham had first surmised on the strength of the topographical indications afforded by ancient writers, was confirmed by the discovery on the part of some villagers of a stone vase in one of

[1] As regards the monuments described by Hsüan Tsang see p. 59 below.

the stūpas[1] near Shāhpur, the inscription on which records that the stūpa in question had been erected at Taxila. Gen. Cunningham's own explorations, which were carried out in the cold seasons of 1863-64 and 1872-73, were limited to mere superficial trenches and pits near the north-east corner of the city of Sirkap, and in some of the isolated mounds on Hathiāl, at Jaṇḍiāl, Mohṛā Maliārāñ, and Seri-ki-Piṇḍ. The only discoveries of any consequence made by him were two temples of inconsiderable size near the village of Mohṛā Maliārāñ,[2] one of which was remarkable for the Ionic columns with which it was adorned. The results of these operations are embodied in Gen. Cunningham's reports for the years 1863-64 and 1872-73. Since the latter date further spoliation among these historic remains has been effected by neighbouring villagers, and numerous antiquities from here have found their way into the hands of the dealers of Rawalpindi. In no case has there been any system or purpose other than that of treasure-seeking in these haphazard excavations, nor has any record of them been preserved.

Of the excavations which the writer has conducted at Taxila during the last four winter seasons, a full and illustrated record is published in his Annual Reports.[3]

[1] No. 13 of Gen. Cunningham's plan in *C. S. R.*, Vol. II, Pl. LXIII.

[2] *A. S. R.*, Vol. V, pp. 68-73 and plates XVII-XIX.

[3] *Annual Reports of the Director General of Archæology*, 1912-13, Pt. I., pp. 8-17, Pt. II., pp. 1-52; 1913-14, Pt. I., pp. 11-17; 1914-15, Pt. I., pp. 13-16, Pt. II., pp. 1-41; 1915-16, Pt. I., pp. 3, 4, 10-12, Pt. II, pp. 1-38.

*Chronology of important events connected with Taxila.*

B.C. 558-529 . Cyrus or Kurush, founder of the Achæmenid Empire of Persia.

563-2 . . Birth of Siddhārtha or Gautama Śākyamuni, the Buddha.

527 . . . Death of Mahāvīra Vardhamāna Jnātaputra, founder of the Jaina religion.
or 467

521-485 . . Darius Hystaspes (Dārayavush Vishtāspa) king of Persia.

Taxila and the north-west of India annexed to the Persian Empire.

Skylax of Karyanda explores the lower course of the Indus (between 515 and 509).

485-465 . . Xerxes (Khshayārshā), king of Persia.

483 . . . Death (*Mahāparinirvāṇa*) of the Buddha.

326 . . . Alexander the Great receives submission of Āmbhi, king of Taxila, and afterwards defeats Porus at the Hydaspes (*Vitastā*-Jihlam).

323 . . . Death of Alexander at Babylon.

321 . . . Second partition of Macedonian Empire at Triparadeisos. Seleucus Nicātōr obtains Babylon, Syria, and Persia; Āmbhi is confirmed in possession of the Hydaspes country; Porus in that of the lower Indus.

317 . . . Eudemus withdraws from the Indus valley, and Chandragupta makes himself master of the Panjab, and founds the Maurya dynasty.

312 . . . (Oct. 1st) Establishment of the Seleucidan era.

305-303 . . Seleucus invades India and is repulsed by Chandragupta.

300 Cir. . . Megasthenes, ambassador of Seleucus, at the court of Chandragupta.

| | |
|---|---|
| 298 . . . | Accession of Bindusāra Maurya. During his reign his son Aśoka is Viceroy at Taxila. Deīmachus, ambassador of Seleucus, at Pāṭaliputra. |
| 273 . . . | Accession of the Emperor Aśoka. |
| 250 Cir. . . | Bactria and Parthia assert their independence. |
| 232 . . . | Death of Aśoka ; break-up of Maurya Empire begins. |
| 190 Cir. . . | Demetrius of Bactria conquers the Panjab. |
| 170-175 . . | Eucratides wrests power from Demetrius, first in Bactria, then in the Panjab. Foundation of the city of Sirkap. |
| 140 Cir. . . | Antialcidas, king of Taxila. Heliodorus sent as ambassador to king of Vidiśā in Central India. |
| 139 Cir. . . | Mithridates of Parthia overthrows kingdom of Bactria. |
| 85-80 . . | Maues, the Scythian king, conquers Taxila. |
| 58 . . . | Beginning of Vikrama era. About this date Azes I succeeds Maues. |
| 17 . . . | Liaka Kusulaka Satrap. |
| 15 Cir. . . | Accession of Azilises. |
| B.C. 10-A.D. 10. | Pātika and Rājūvula Satraps. |
| B.C. 5 Cir. . | Accession of Azes II. |
| A.D. 20-30 . | Kingdoms of Arachosia and Taxila united under one rule by Parthian Gondopharnes. |
| 35 Cir. . . | Conquest of Kābul valley from Hermæus by Gondopharnes. |
| 40 Cir. . . | Visit of St. Thomas the Apostle to the court of Gondopharnes. |
| 44 . . . | Visit of Apollonius of Tyāna. Phraotes ruling at Taxila. |

| | |
|---|---|
| 50-60 . . | Death of Gondopharnes and division of empire among various Parthian princes, including Abdagases, Orthagnes, Pakores, Sasan, Sapedanes, etc. |
| 60 Cir. . . | Hermæus and Kujūla Kadphises reconquer Kābul valley and afterwards annex Gandhāra and Taxila. |
| 75-80 Cir.. . | Accession of Wima Kadphises, the Kushān king. |
| 100 " . . | 'Soter Megas.' |
| 125 " . . | Accession of Kanishka Kushān. Foundation of the city of Sirsukh. |
| 146 " . . | Arrian, author of the *Indika*, flourished. |
| 170 " . . | Accession of Huvishka. |
| 187 " . . | Accession of Vāsudeva. |
| 225 " . . | Death of Vāsudeva and break-up of Kushān power. |
| 226 . . . | Ardashīr-i-Bābegān founded the Sasanian dynasty of Persia. |
| 319 . . . | Chandragupta I, founder of the Imperial Gupta dynasty, crowned. Gupta era begins. |
| 400 . . . | Fa Hien, the Chinese pilgrim, visits Taxila. |
| 430 . . . | Kidāra Shāhi establishes the kingdom of the Little Kushāns. |
| 450-500 . . | Invasions of Ephthalites or White Huns and expulsion of Little Kushāns from Gandhāra. |
| 510 Cir. . . | Death of Toramāṇa and accession of Mihiragula. |
| 520 . . . | Sung Yün, the Chinese pilgrim, in Gandhāra. |
| 629-645 . . | Hsüan Tsang, the Chinese pilgrim, visits India. |

## CHAPTER III

### ART[1]

We have seen in the foregoing chapter that between the fifth century B.C. and the fifth century A.D. Taxila was under the dominion, successively, of seven different nations, namely: the Persians, the Macedonians, the Mauryas, the Bactrian Greeks, the Scythians (Śakas), the Parthians and the Kushāns; and it may be taken for granted that, with the exception of the Macedonians whose conquest was merely transitory, each of these nations in turn left some impress upon the arts and culture of the country. Of artistic monuments ACHÆMENIAN. however, belonging to the Persian epoch none have yet been found either at Taxila or elsewhere in India, and, indeed, the only relic of any kind in which direct Achæmenian influence is discernible, is the Aramaic inscription mentioned on p. 75. True, there are strong Persian elements observable in the sculptures of a later epoch, particularly in those of the Gandhāra school, and it has generally been assumed that these elements found their way into Indian art at the time

[1] For a fuller account of the evolution of early Indian art, see the writer's chapters in the forthcoming *Cambridge History of India*, some paragraphs from which are here repeated.

when the Persian Empire extended over the north-west, the Greek elements following later. There is no real evidence, however, to support this assumption. A more reasonable view is that the fusion of Iranian with Hellenistic ideas took place in Bactria and the neighbouring countries after their colonisation by Alexander the Great, and that the hybrid art there evolved was introduced into India either as a result of the peaceful intercourse between the Maurya Empire and Western Asia, or as a result of the subsequent invasions of the Bactrian Greeks, Scythians, Parthians, and Kushāns, all of whom must have been imbued to a greater or less degree with Græco-Persian culture.

MAURYA. Whatever the truth may be regarding an earlier stratum of Achæmenian art in the North-West, the history of Indian art at present opens for us in the Maurya age, when indigenous art had not yet emerged from the primitive stage, and when the Emperor Aśoka was employing artists from Bactria or its neighbourhood for the erection of his famous memorials. The rudimentary character of Indian art at this period is well exemplified by the current indigenous coins (Pl. II) known commonly as 'punch-marked,' which are singularly crude and ugly, neither their form, which is unsymmetrical, nor the symbols which are stamped almost indiscriminately upon their surface, having any pretensions to artistic merit. On the other hand, the coins of Sophytes (Saubhūti), who was reigning in the Salt Range at the close of the 4th century B.C., are purely Greek in style (Pl. II), having seemingly been copied from an issue of Seleucus Nicātōr, with whom Sophytes probably came into

1 & 2. *PUNCH-MARKED.*

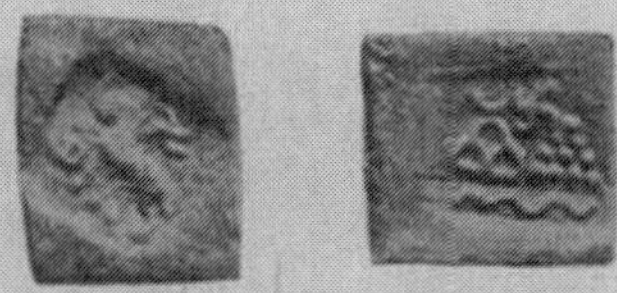

3 & 4. *LOCAL TAXILAN.*

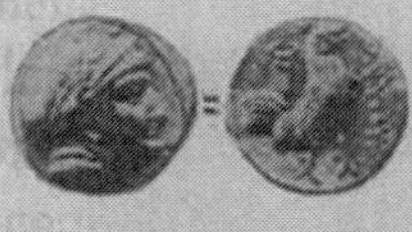

5. *SOPHYTES.*

6. *DIODOTUS.*

7. *EUTHYDEMUS.*

8. *DEMETRIUS.*

9. *PANTALEON.*

10. *EUCRATIDES.*

11. *ANTIALCIDAS.*

12. *APOLLODOTUS.*

13. *MENANDER.*

contact when the former invaded the Panjab. This striking contrast between indigenous and foreign workmanship is no less apparent in the plastic art of the period. Thus, side by side with the masterly figures, both in the round and in relief, with which some of the columns of Aśoka are crowned and which are manifestly the products of the highly mature Perso-Greek School, there are images, such as the one from Pārkham in the Mathura Museum, which are still in the unifacial and frontal stage and exhibit all the other defects of rudimentary technique. Indeed, so far as is known at present, it was only in the jewellers' and lapidaries' arts that the Maurya craftsman attained any real proficiency, and in this domain his aptitude lay, not in the plastic treatment of form, but in the highly technical skill with which he cut and polished refractory stones or applied delicate filigree or granular designs to metal objects. The refined quality of his gold and silver work is well illustrated in the two pieces reproduced in Pl. XVI, 13 and 14, which were discovered in the Bhiṛ mound in company with a gold coin of Diodotus, a large number of local punch-marked coins and a quantity of other jewellery and precious stones. Apart from this jewellery, almost every object hitherto recovered from the Maurya stratum at Taxila is of rough, primitive workmanship, and the same is true of the majority of contemporary objects from other sites.

GREEK, SCYTHIC AND PARTHIAN.

Of the Greek kings of the Panjab, our knowledge is, as we saw in the last chapter, very limited, and is in fact mainly derived from their coins, which are found in large numbers throughout the Panjab and North-West Frontier. From these coins we have recovered the names of some 40 kings, but of the majority little more is known than their actual names. The only record, on stone, of these Greek kings is one which was found a thousand miles away from Taxila in the ancient city of Vidiśā in Central India. This inscription is carved on a pillar, and states that the pillar was set up by a Greek named Heliodorus, the son of Dion, who came as ambassador to Vidiśā from Antialcidas, the Greek king of Taxila. Incidentally, this inscription shows us how the Greeks were then embracing the religions of the country of their adoption. With their very elastic pantheon they readily identified Indian gods with their own deities; and, just as in Italy they identified Minerva with Athena or Bacchus with Dionysus, so in India they identified the Sun-god Sūrya with Apollo or Kāma, the god of Love, with their own Eros; and they had no hesitation, therefore, in paying their devotions to Śiva or to Pārvatī, to Vishṇu or to Lakshmī.

The North-West of India, which the Greeks occupied, has been swept by invasion after invasion of hosts from Central Asia, and there are relatively few monuments of ancient days that have escaped destruction. Those, however, which have survived, as well as the monuments and antiquities that have recently been recovered from the soil at Taxila and other places, all consistently bear witness to the strong hold which Hellenistic art took upon this part of India. This hold was so strong, that long after the Greek kingdoms of the Panjab had passed away, even after the Scythians and Parthians, who overthrew the Greeks, had themselves been supplanted by the Kushāns, Greek art still remained paramount in the North-West, and continued to exercise considerable influence until the fifth century of our era, although it was growing more and more decadent year by year.

This persistence and this slow decadence of Greek ideas is best illustrated by the coins, the stylistic history of which is singularly lucid and coherent (Pls. II and III). In the earliest examples every feature is Hellenistic. The standard weight of the coins is the standard established by Athens; the legends are in Greek; the types are taken from Greek mythology, and are moreover designed with a grace and beauty reminiscent of the schools of Praxiteles and Lysippus; and their portraiture is characterised by a refined realism which, while it is unmistakably Greek, demonstrates a remarkable originality on the part of the engravers in India. Later on, when the Greek power in India became consolidated, the old Attic standard gave place to one, possibly based on Persian coinage, which was more suited to the needs of local commerce; bilingual legends (on the one side in Greek, on the other in Kharoshṭhī) were substituted for the Greek; and little by little the other Greek qualities gradually faded, Indian elements being introduced among the types and the portraits losing their freshness and animation. And so the process of degeneration continued, relatively slowly among the Eurasian Greeks, more rapidly when the Greeks were supplanted by the Scythians and Parthians. The testimony of these coins is especially valuable in this respect: it proves that the engravers who produced them were no mere slavish copyists of western models, but were giving free and spontaneous expression to their own ideas; and it proves further that, though Greek art underwent an inevitable transformation on Indian soil, and as a result of political changes, nevertheless its influence was long and well sustained.

The same is the case also with the engraved gems, which are found in large numbers throughout the Panjab and North-West Frontier and which exhibit precisely the same stylistic development as the coins. Nor does this numismatic and glyptic evidence stand alone. It is endorsed also by the other antiquities of this age which have come down to us, though in their case with this notable difference—a difference for which political considerations readily account—that, whereas the coins of the Indo-Parthians evince a close dependence on Parthian prototypes, warranting the presumption that the kings who issued them were of Parthian stock, the contemporary architecture and other antiquities show relatively little evidence of the semi-barbarous influence from that region. Of the buildings of the Eurasian Greeks themselves no remains have yet been brought to light save the plain and unembellished dwelling houses of Taxila, but the monuments erected on this site during the Scytho-Parthian supremacy leave no room for doubt that architecture of the classical style had long been fashionable in this quarter of India; for, though by that time the decorative features were beginning to be Indianised, the Hellenistic elements in them were still in complete preponderance over the Oriental. Thus, the ornamentation of the stūpas of this period was primarily based on the "Corinthian" order, modified by the addition of Indian motifs,

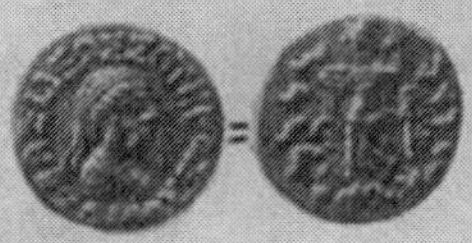

14. *ZOILUS.*

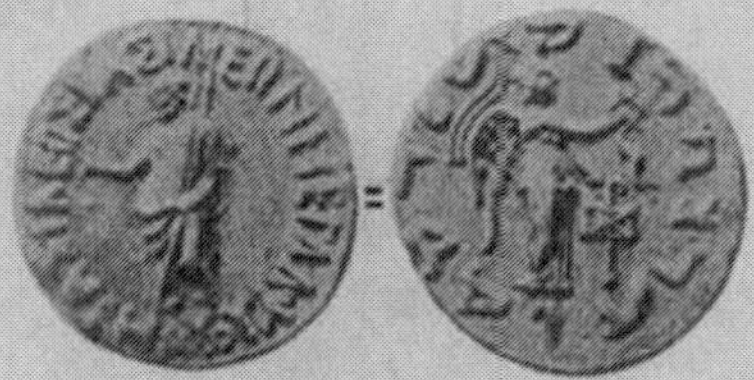

15. *MAUES.*

16. *AZES I.*

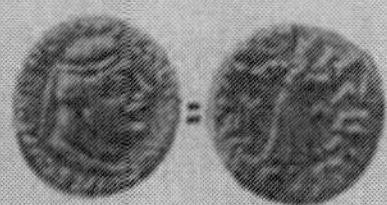

17. *RAJUVULA.*

18. *GONDOPHARNES.*

19. *HERMAEUS.*

20. *KADPHISES II.*

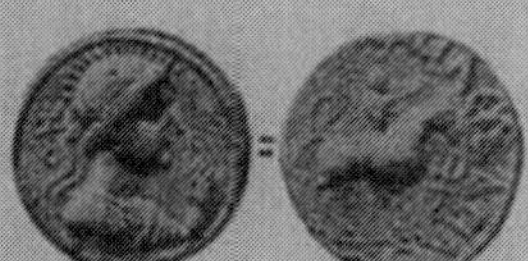

21. *BASILEUS MEGAS.*

22. *KANISHKA.*

23. *VASUDEVA.*

while the only temples that have yet been unearthed are characterised by the presence of Ionic columns and classical mouldings. In the example of the former class of structures illustrated in Pl. XII the Indian elements in the design are more than usually conspicuous, but even in this stūpa, which belongs to the reign of Azes and probably to the Jaina faith, they are restricted to the small brackets over the Corinthian capitals and to the subsidiary *toraṇas*[1] and arched niches which relieve the interspaces between the pilasters.

As with the architectural, so with the plastic and other arts; they, one and all, derived their inspiration from the Hellenistic School and in the very slowness of their decline, bear testimony to the remarkable persistency of its teachings. Of earlier and purer workmanship a good illustration is afforded by the ivory pendant adorned with two bearded heads from Sirkap (Pl. XVI, 10) and by the vine-wreathed head of Dionysus in silver repoussé from the same spot (Pl. I). The god is garlanded with the usual vine, has the Satyr's ears, and carries in his hands a typical double-handled *cantharus*. The style of this head is bold and broad, and characteristic of the best period of Hellenistic art. To a little later date—probably the first century B.C.—belongs the beautiful little statuette of bronze figured in Pl. XV. It is the figure of Harpocrates, the Egyptian child god of silence, and

[1] The finest and indeed the only complete examples of ancient Indian *toraṇas* (gateways) are those at Sāñchī in Bhopal State. The Indian *toraṇa* is the prototype of the Chinese "pailu" and the Japanese "torii." No doubt it was introduced into those countries with the spread of Buddhism to the East.

it is in token of silence that he holds his finger to his lips. There is a charming simplicity and naïveté about the treatment of this child, which is unmistakably Greek. Later on (that is to say, about the beginning of the Christian era) we find Indian ideas beginning to coalesce with the Greek and art becoming somewhat more hybrid. Witness, for example, the well known gold casket from Bimārān[1] in Afghanistan, in which the figures of the Buddha and his devotees (the chief and central figures) are in inspiration clearly Hellenic, but the arches under which they stand are no less clearly Indian; while beneath the base of the casket is the sacred Indian lotus, full blown.

Under the supremacy of the Kushāns a vast number of Buddhist monasteries and stūpas sprang into existence, and a new lease of life was given to the old Greek School. No doubt, during their long sojourn in Bactria and the Oxus Valley the Kushāns had absorbed much of the Oriental Greek spirit, and it was probably due to this that their arrival in India was the signal for a fresh outburst of artistic activity. The chief centre of this activity was the valley of Peshawar, where Kanishka established his winter capital. This tract of

GANDHĀRAN. country was then called Gandhāra, and it is for this reason that the school of art which flourished here during the Kushān epoch is known as the Gandhāra School. Large collections of the sculptures which this school produced have been made on the frontier, and

[1] *Cf. Ariana Antiqua*, p. 53, Pl. III; Foucher, *L'Art gréco-bouddhique du Gandhāra*, p. 51, fig. 7; Birdwood, *Industrial Arts of India*, Pl. I; Vincent Smith, *History of fine Art in India and Ceylon*, p. 356 and Pl. LXXIV, fig. B.

may be seen in the museums at Peshawar, Lahore and Calcutta; numerous specimens, too, have been found at Taxila itself, of which some illustrations are given on Pl. VIII.[1] Unhappily, among the many thousands of sculptures of this school which we possess, there is not one which bears a date in any known era, nor do considerations of style enable us to determine their chronological sequence with any approach to accuracy. Nevertheless, it may be taken as a general maxim that the earlier they are, the more nearly they approximate in style to Hellenistic work, and it may also be safely asserted that a number of them, distinguished by their less stereotyped or less rococo character, are anterior to the reign of Kanishka.

The sculptures of this school were executed in stone,[2] stucco, and terracotta and appear to have been invariably embellished with gold leaf or paint. Stone being the more durable, it happens that most of the specimens preserved at Peshawar, Lahore, and in other museums are in that material; but at Taxila we have been fortunate in recovering, besides stone images, a vast number of well-preserved stucco ones and a few also in terracotta.

In many features, both of style and execution, these sculptures recall to mind Roman work of the same period, and this resemblance has led some writers to suppose that Roman art and Roman culture extended their influence as far as Northern India. This ex-

[1] *Cf.* also pp. 55, 56 below.

[2] The stone used for most of these sculptures is a peculiar variety of grey schist stone, which is believed to come from the neighbourhood of the Swat Valley, though its provenance has never been definitely settled.

planation, however, is based on a fundamental error as to the genesis of Roman Imperial art and the relation in which it stood to the Hellenistic art of Western Asia. Ever since the time of the Seleucids it was Western Asia that had been the real centre of artistic effort in the ancient world. Western Asia was the crucible in which the arts of Greece and of Ionia, of Persia and of Mesopotamia, were fused together; and it was from Western Asia that the streams of art flowed westward over the Roman Empire and eastward over Parthia, Turkestan and India. It is a mistake to suppose that Roman ideas affected to any great extent the plastic arts of Greece or Asia. The converse was the case, and the art of Rome, therefore, stood in much the same relation as the art of Gandhāra did to Hellenistic art. In other words, Gandhāra art was the sister (or more correctly, perhaps the cousin), not the daughter, of Roman art, both schools tracing their parentage to the same common stock; and it is not surprising, therefore, to find that the arts of Rome and of Gandhāra are distinguished by the same family likenesses.

**Influence of Greek art in India.**

The question of the rôle played by classical art in India has been a much disputed one in the past, some authorities maintaining that it was almost a negligible factor, others that it underlay the whole fabric of Indian art. The truth, as so often happens, lies between the two extremes. In Hindustan and in Central India it played an important part in promoting the development of the Early National School, both by clearing its path of technical difficulties and strengthening its growth with new and invigorating ideas. In the north-west region and immediately beyond its frontiers, on the other hand, it long maintained a complete supremacy, obscuring the indigenous traditions and itself producing works of no mean merit, which add appreciably to our understanding of the Hellenistic genius. Here, too, as Indian influence waxed stronger, it eventually culminated in the School of Gandhāra, which left an indelible mark on Buddhist art throughout the Orient. Nevertheless, in spite of its wide diffusion, Hellenistic art never took the real hold upon India that it took, for example, upon Italy or Western Asia, for the reason that the temperaments of the two peoples were radically dissimilar. To the Greek, man, man's beauty, man's intellect were everything, and it was the apotheosis of this beauty and this intellect which still remained the keynote of Hellenistic art even in the Orient. But these ideals awakened no response in the Indian mind. The vision of the Indian was bounded by the immortal rather than the mortal, by the infinite rather than the finite. Where Greek thought was ethical, his was spiritual ; where Greek was rational, his was emotional. And to these higher aspirations, these more spiritual instincts, he sought, at a later date, to give articulate expression by translating them into terms of form and colour. But that was not until the more spacious times of the Guptas, when a closer contact had been established between thought and art, and new impulses imparted to each. Prior to the mediæval epoch the Indian had not conceived the bold and, as some think, chimerical idea of thus incarnating spirit in matter. Art to him was a thing apart—a sensuous, concrete expression of the beautiful, which appealed intimately to his subconscious æsthetic sense, but in which neither intellectuality nor mysticism had any share. For the rest, he found in the formative arts a valuable medium in which to narrate, in simple and universal language, the legends and history of his faith; and this was mainly why, for the sake of its lucidity and dramatic power, he welcomed and absorbed the lessons of Hellenistic art, not because he sympathised with its ideals or saw in it the means of giving utterance to his own.

## .CHAPTER IV

### THE DHARMARĀJIKĀ STŪPA[1]

In the description which follows of the remains of Taxila[2] I shall start with the Dharmarājikā Stūpa,

[1] Primarily stūpas were, no doubt, funeral mounds or tumuli; but among the Buddhists they were erected either to enshrine some relic of the Buddha or of a Buddhist saint or else to commemorate some specially sacred spot. From the outward form of a stūpa it is not possible to determine whether it contains a relic or not. The erection of a stūpa has always been regarded by the Buddhists as a work of merit, which brings its author a step nearer to salvation. "Tope" is a corrupt Anglo-Indian word derived from *thūpa*, the Prakrit form of *stūpa*. In Burma a stūpa is commonly known as a '*pagoda*' and in Ceylon as a '*dāgaba*'—a Singalese word derived from '*dhātu*'=a 'relic' and '*garbha*'=receptacle or shrine. In Nepal it is called a *chaitya*, a word which, like stūpa, originally meant a heap or tumulus (*chitā*) but subsequently came to mean a sanctuary of any kind. See Fergusson, *I. E. A.*, pp. 54-5; *C. I. I.*, Vol. III, p. 30, Note I. For the details of the construction and dedication of a stūpa see *Mahāvaṃśa*, 169 sqq; *Divyāvadāna*, p. 244; Cunningham, *Bhilsa Topes*, Ch. XIII; H. A. Oldfield, *Sketches from Nepal*, II, pp. 210-12; Foucher, *L'Art Gréco-Bouddhique*, pp. 94-98.

[2] To visit all the remains now brought to light at Taxila two full days are required. At present the roads are unmetalled, and, except in good weather and when they have recently been repaired, are not suitable for motor cars. A 'Bareilly' cart can generally be obtained at Sarai-kala, but it is advisable to arrange for it in advance. In this and other matters the overseer at the Archæological bungalow gives whatever assistance he can. Assuming that a visitor has only five or six hours to spare, a good plan is to drive to the Dharmarājikā stūpa (Chir Tope), thence walk (about a mile and a quarter) through a defile in the hills to the stūpa of Kunāla, and afterwards descend into the city of Sirkap. The conveyance can

then proceed over the ridge of Hathiāl to the stūpa of Kunāla and descend from there into the city of Sirkap. From Sirkap I shall conduct the visitor over the temple at Jaṇḍiāl and the remains of two small stūpas beyond it to the north. Thence we shall make our way to the city of Sirsukh and the Buddhist monuments at Lālchak and Bādalpur; and finally we shall visit what are in some respects the most remarkable and the best preserved of all the monuments at Taxila, namely, the Buddhist stūpas and monasteries at Mohṛā Morādu and Jauliāñ.

The Dharmarājikā stūpa or 'Chir Tope'[1] (Pl. IX), as it is locally known from the cleft driven through its centre by former explorers, stands on a lofty plateau high above the Tamrā nālā. Prior to the spot being occupied by a Buddhist establishment, it appears to have been the site of a village. To this early stratum of habitation belongs a collection of 28 coins of the Greek king Zoilus, which were unearthed below the foundation of the building H. The Great Stūpa, which stands in the centre of the plateau, is much ruined—so much so that fifty years ago Sir Alexander Cunningham affirmed that only the core of the structure survived. The recent excavations, however, in the course of which

meanwhile go round to the northern side of Sirkap and having rejoined it the visitor can drive to the Temple of Jaṇḍiāl and thence to Mohṛā Morādu and Jauliāñ. The antiquities at the Archæological Bungalow should, when accessible to visitors, be seen after rather than before the monuments.

[1] The unmetalled road that has been made to the Dharmarājikā stūpa is a winding one and nearly two miles long. There is a short cut across the Tamrā nālā immediately to the east of the Bhiṛ mound.

PLAN OF THE DHARMARAJIKA STŪPA. PLATE IV.

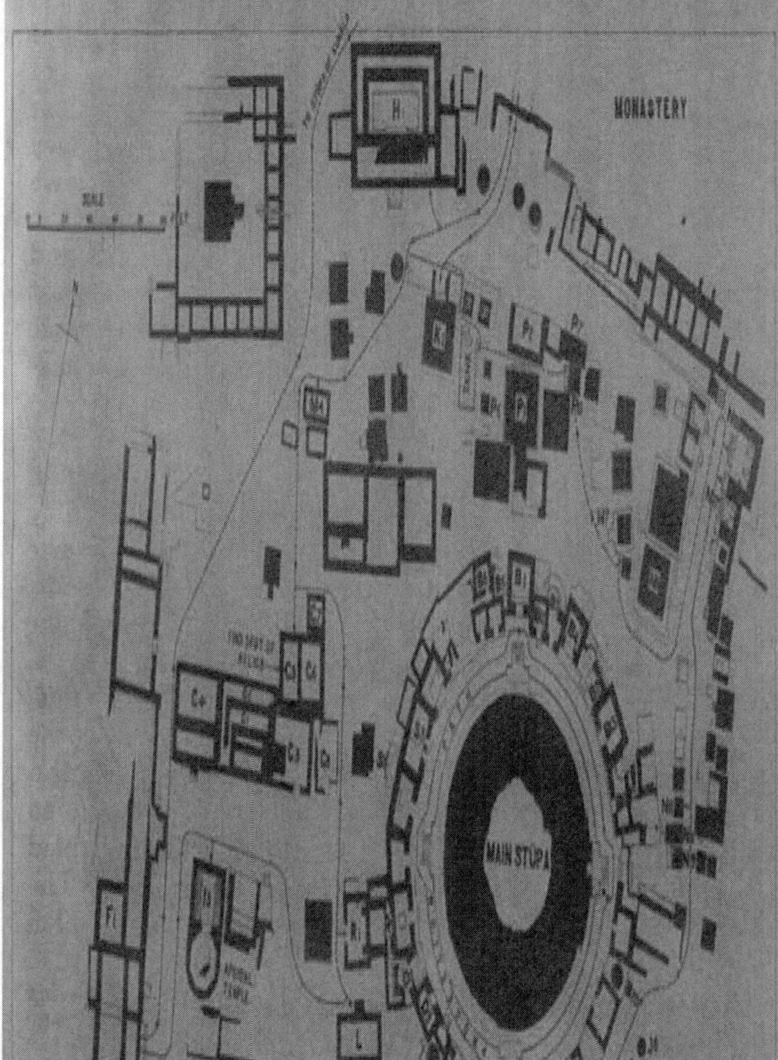

débris to the depth of some thirty feet has been removed from around its base, have revealed considerable sections of the old facing in a fair state of preservation, and have brought to light a large number of other interesting structures, including stūpas, chapels and monastic quarters, which, extending as they do over a period of at least four centuries, furnish us with important data for the history of local architecture. Thanks, also, to the coins and other minor antiquities found in association with them, they help us materially towards the solution of many chronological problems connected with this period of ancient history.

THE MAIN STRUCTURE

The main structure, as now exposed, is circular in plan with a raised terrace around its base, which was ascended by four flights of steps, one at each of the cardinal points. The core of the stūpa is of rough rubble masonry strengthened by walls, between 3 and 5 feet in thickness, radiating from the centre. These construction walls stop short above the berm of the stūpa, instead of being carried down to its foundations, and appear to belong to a subsequent reconstruction of the fabric, which took place probably during the Kushān epoch. The outer facing is of ponderous limestone blocks with chiselled kañjūr stone let in between them for the mouldings and pilasters, the whole having been once finished with a coating of lime plaster and paint. The ornamental stone carving on the face of the stūpa above the berm is best preserved on the eastern side. Its most distinguishing features are the boldness of its mouldings and the design of its niches, which are framed alternately by trefoil arches and doorways with sloping jambs, and divided one from the other by Corinthian pilasters. The same type of decoration is also found on smaller stūpas on this site belonging to the 3rd, 4th and 5th centuries A.D. Apparently, the original stūpa was built in the time of the Scytho-Parthian rulers, but repaired and enlarged in the Kushān epoch and partly refaced again about the 4th century A.D., to which period the decoration above the terrace belongs.

The raised terrace and the open passage around the foot of the stūpa served in ancient days as procession paths (*pradakshiṇa patha*), round which it was customary for the faithful to 'process,' keeping the stūpa always on the right hand. Now-a-days, the Buddhists ordinarily process three times round a stūpa or other sacred edifice, but in obedience to vows they will process 7, 14 or even 108 times.

The original floor of the procession path is composed of lime mixed with river sand, and part of it in the north-west quadrant is adorned in a curious fashion with shell bangles imbedded in the plaster and arranged in various geometrical designs, some of the bangles being whole, others cut in halves or in quarters.[1] Above this floor was an accumulation of débris about three inches thick and over this, again, a second *chunam* floor. In the stratum immediately above this latter floor were found many pieces of glass tiles. Probably, the whole of the procession path was at one time paved with these glass tiles, and later on, when the pavement had fallen into disrepair, a number of the tiles were removed

[1] For the protection of this decoration, it has for the time being been covered again with a layer of earth.

from here to the chamber $F^1$, where they were found laid in a somewhat careless manner.[1]

Immediately to the left of the steps on the eastern side of the stūpa is the lower part of a pillar, which probably once supported a lion capital, like the pillars in Sirkap (p. 75). Such pillars were doubtless imitated from the well known pillars of Aśoka, which were frequently set up beside important Buddhist stūpas.

Of the minor antiquities found in the procession passage the only ones of interest were some Gandhāra sculptures and coins. Of the former a typical specimen is a figure of the Bodhisattva[2] (?Śākyamuni) standing beneath an umbrella canopy in the attitude of protection (*abhaya-mudrā*), with attendant figures. The coins were found in a hoard to the number of 355 concealed in a small block of kañjūr stone near the western steps. They comprise specimens of Azes II, Soter Megas, Huvishka, Vāsudeva and issues of Indo-Sasanian or Kushāno-Sasanian type.

SMALL CIRCULAR STŪPAS AROUND THE MAIN STRUCTURE.

The Great Stūpa described above was, it need hardly be said, the first of the Buddhist structures to be erected on the plateau. At the time when it was constructed, the plateau around was levelled

[1] *A. S. R.* 1912-13, Pt. II, p. 18.

[2] Bodhisattva means literally a being whose characteristic (*sattva*=Pāli *satta*) and aim are enlightenment (*bodhi*). Gautama was a Bodhisattva in his previous existence and also during his historical existence up to the time when he attained enlightenment, and became the Buddha. According to the Northern or Mahāyāna School of Buddhism, there are besides Gautama innumerable other Bodhisattvas, both human and divine, among the best known of whom are: Avalokiteśvara, Mañjuśrī, Mārichi and Samantabhadra, Vajrapāṇi and Maitreya, the last of whom is the coming and last Buddha of this age of the world.

up and covered with a layer of grey river sand with a floor of lime plaster above. On this floor or on the débris which accumulated immediately above it there was subsequently built, in a ring around the central edifice, a number of small stūpas, of which ten have been unearthed up to date. In the plan on Pl. IV they are numbered, starting from the west, $R^4$, $S^8$, $B^6$, $B^3$, $B^7$, $B^{16}$, $B^{20}$, $D^{10}$, $D^1$, $D^2$ and $D^3$. These small stūpas were originally circular in plan and constructed of rough rubble cores generally faced with square kañjūr blocks, the only existing decoration being a simple base moulding. Later on, several of them, *e.g.*, $D^3$, and $R^4$, were enlarged by the addition of square bases. In several of these stūpas, buried at a depth of five or six feet beneath their bases, were found relic deposits of which the two following may be taken as typical examples.

In $B^6$ the relic chamber, roughly constructed of small stones and covered by a large slab of limestone,[1] contained a casket of steatite and a miniature stūpa of fine grey limestone. Inside the casket, which is 4 in. high and well-turned on the lathe, was a smaller casket of silvery bronze $1\frac{3}{8}$ in. high, in the form of a stūpa crowned with umbrellas; and in this miniature receptacle were some calcined bones and ashes, and a few gold, agate, pearl and bone beads. The stūpa of grey limestone is provided with a small cavity underneath, in which were packed together a large assortment of interesting beads and gems of the following materials:—ruby, crystal, banded agate,

[1] This stupa is no longer exposed to view.

jacinth, sard, garnet, amethyst, cornelian, aquamarine, green jasper, onyx, mother-of-pearl, glass, topaz and bone. Some of these beads are in the shape of animals or birds, such as the lion, tortoise, frog and goose; others are in the form of a crescent or *triratna*[1]; others are barrel shaped, polygonal or amygdaloid. From the appearance of the little limestone stūpa it may be surmised that it formerly belonged to an older structure, and that it was transferred to the one in which I found it when its original resting place had fallen into disrepair. Whether the gems inside it were of the same date or not, is open to question.

In the relic chamber of another stūpa ($S^8$) were four small earthenware lamps—one in each corner of the chamber—four coins of the Scythian kings, Maues and Azes I, and a vase of steatite. The vase contained a miniature casket of gold together with three gold safety pins, and some small beads of ruby, garnet, amethyst, and crystal; and inside the miniature gold casket, again, were some beads of bone and ruby with pieces of silver leaf, coral and stone, and along with these the bone relic. In February, 1917, these relics were presented by the Viceroy, Lord Chelmsford, to the Buddhists of Ceylon and were enshrined by them in the Temple of the Tooth Relic (Dalada Maligawa) at Kandy.

CIRCLE OF SMALL CHAPELS.

The next stage of building around the Great Stūpa is marked by the erection of gateways opposite the steps at the four cardinal points, and of a circle of

[1] *Triratna*='Three jewels.' The trident device symbolises the trinity of Buddhism: the Buddha, the Dharma (Law) and the Saṅgha (Religious order).

small chapels which are similar in plan, as well in purpose, to those at Jamālgaṛhī in the Frontier Province, being intended for the enshrinement of Buddhist images which were set up facing the Great Stūpa. In Burma, it is against the Buddhist principles ever to destroy a stūpa or any other work of merit, and it may be presumed that the same practice obtained among the Buddhists of ancient India. Accordingly, when these chapels were built, the small stūpas then standing, although much decayed, were suffered to remain, the ground between them being partially filled in with débris and the walls of the new chapels carried over their tops.

CONSECUTIVE TYPES OF MASONRY.

The earliest of these chapels as well as the walls flanking the gateways, which date from the latter half of the first century A.D., are built in a very distinctive style of masonry known commonly as 'diaper patterned'. At the period to which they belong the diaper was characterised by the use of relatively small boulders and by the neatness of the piles of small stones in the interstices between them. Examples of this masonry can be seen in the chapels numbered $B^{12}$, $B^{16}$, $D^{9}$.

About the close of the first century A.D. this small diaper masonry gave place to a new type in which larger boulders were employed. This is the third distinct style of masonry employed on this site. It is found in repairs executed to the original chapels as well as in several chapels which were afterwards added, and is well exemplified in the chambers $D^{5}$ and $D^{8}$. With the lapse of time the buildings in which it was employed in turn fell to ruin, the

PLATE V.

1. *RUBBLE.*

2. *SMALL DIAPER.*

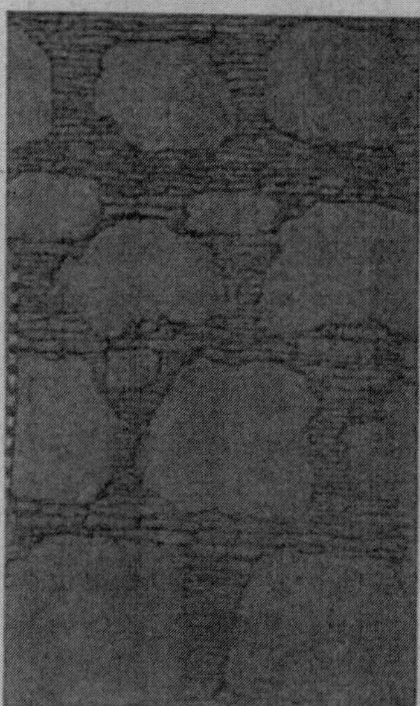

3. *LARGE DIAPER.*

4. *SEMI-ASHLAR.*

spaces between became filled with fallen débris, and over this (at a height, that is to say, of several feet above the original floor) were constructed other chapels in still another kind of masonry. This fourth variety is characterised by the use of ashlar and diaper masonry combined, and appears to have been in vogue in the 3rd, 4th and 5th centuries A.D. It is used for the repair of the upper parts of the earlier chapels as well as in the construction of new ones, *e.g.*, $B^1$, and $B^{13}$. In the earlier examples of this semi-ashlar masonry a single course of ashlar is inserted between the larger boulders; in the later examples the single course is replaced by two or even three courses.

Thus, we have four clear and distinct types of masonry immediately around the Main Stūpa (Pl. V): first, the rubble and *kañjūr* work of the Scytho-Parthian period; secondly, the neat small diaper which came into fashion in the 1st century A.D.; thirdly, the coarse and massive diaper of the 2nd century A.D.; and fourthly, the semi-ashlar, semi-diaper type of the 3rd and later centuries. These four consecutive types are equally well illustrated in other buildings at the Dharmarājikā Stūpa as well as in Sirkap and other places.

MINOR ANTIQUITIES FROM CHAPELS ROUND MAIN STŪPA.

The antiquities found in these chapels came mainly from the highest stratum and consist for the most part of stucco and terracotta figures, of which typical examples are illustrated in Pl. VI *b* and *c*.

(*b*) Terracotta head, 11½ in. high. The modelling of the features and treatment of the hair is singularly reminiscent of Hellenistic work. Though found in a late stratum from B12, this head was probably executed in the first or second century A.D. (Pl. VI*b*).

(*c*) Stucco head of Bodhisattva, 9 in. high. The hair is disposed in strands falling from the *ushṇīsha*[1] and ending in curls suggestive of bronze technique. From B12 (Pl. VI*c*).

In chapel S3, in its south-west corner, are the remains of a raised platform, the body of which is composed of mud. Buried in the mud were found a large number of clay sealings impressed with the Buddhist creed—*Ye dharmā hetu prabhavā*, etc.,—in characters of the Gupta age. Such seals are frequently found imbedded in ancient Buddhist stūpas and even in statues.

The visitor who has followed the route indicated on the plan in dotted lines will have entered the procession path by its southern entrance, will have performed the *pradakshiṇa* around the Great Stūpa, and will now emerge again by way of the same entrance. As he turns to the left, he will see near by and on his

STŪPA J. right hand a stūpa of considerable size designated J1 in the plan. It consists of a square base, 32 ft. 4 in. square, composed of three tiers which diminish in size as they rise. Above this base was formerly a circular drum and dome crowned by an umbrella, but all traces of these features have now vanished. This stūpa appears to have undergone extensive repairs in the old days, and the decoration that remains is of two different periods. To the earlier period belongs the decoration of the lowest tier on the north

[1] *Ushṇīsha*=protuberance on the crown of the head, one of the marks of a great man (*mahāpurusha*).

(a)

(b)

(c)

(d)

*TERRACOTTA AND STUCCO HEADS FROM THE DHARMARAJIKA STUPA.*

side, consisting of groups of figures separated from one another by debased Corinthian pilasters. The figures are executed in stucco, with which material the whole face of the stūpa was finished off, and represent seated Buddhas accompanied by a devotee standing on either side, whose attire is distinctively Indo-Scythic. When the stūpa was repaired, these groups of figures had already suffered damage, and the frieze above them was then lowered from its position over the capitals of the pilasters, and set in a line with them, thus resting on the shoulders of the Buddhas from which the heads had disappeared. At the same time a new series of pilasters was introduced on the eastern and southern façades of a more stunted form and surmounted with notched brackets let in between the capitals and the frieze. On these two sides there are no Buddhas.

The decoration on the second tier appears to belong to the later repair. It consists of a row of elephants alternating with pairs of Atlantes, the grotesque attitudes and late and decadent modelling of which are noteworthy.

STŪPA $J^2$.

A little further eastward is the stūpa $J^2$, in which some relics of interest were found. The relic chamber was at a height of 2 feet above the floor level and in the centre of the structure. In it was a steatite casket shaped like a Greek *pyxis*, which contained a small box of silver; and in this, again, was a still smaller box of gold containing some minute fragments of bone. There were also a few beads in the steatite casket, but no coins with which to fix its date. The shape of the steatite casket closely resembles that of a casket discovered by the writer some years ago in G̲haz Ḍherī at Charsadda, which was accompanied by a coin of Zeionises[1]; but the mouldings and other decorative features of $J^2$ bespeak for it a much later date than that of Zeionises.

STŪPAS $N^{9-13}$. Passing by the stūpas $J^{3-6}$ and proceeding in a northerly direction, we come to another group of similar monuments, all of which are built in the semi-ashlar type of masonry, are square in plan, and standing to a height of some three feet or less. In the centre of $N^{11}$ was found a large earthen *ghaṛā* of plain red earthenware containing fifteen copper coins of Shapur II (309-379 A.D.). Another earthenware vessel which was discovered in Stūpa $N^{10}$ had been badly crushed, but the earth from it yielded 18 beads of coral, lapis-lazuli, shell and glass. The Stūpa $N^9$ yielded a few beads only.

A little further on is a wide passage flanked on either side by stūpas and chapels and leading to other chapels and also, no doubt, to the monastic quarters (not yet excavated) on the north. Of the chapels

CHAPELS $N^{17}$ AND $N^{18}$. alongside this passage, the two numbered $N^{17}$ and $N^{18}$ are still quite imposing even in their ruin. They are constructed of massive semi-ashlar masonry and date from the fourth or fifth century A.D. Inside are the remains of several images of Buddha, of which the principal ones facing the entrances were of colossal proportions. Of the one in $N^{18}$ only the feet and lower part of the raiment have survived, but the size of the former (5 ft. 3 in. from heel to toe) indicate

[1] *A. S. R.*, 1902-03, Pt. II, pp. 175-176.

that the figure had an approximate height of 35 feet; and it follows, therefore, that the chapel itself must have been hardly less than 40 feet high. The core of these images, as of others of the same age, is composed either of kañjūr stone roughly fashioned to the shape of the figure, or of mud, or of mud and stones combined; the stucco coating in which the features and other details are made out, is almost pure lime. In several instances red paint is still adhering to the robes of the statues, and no doubt other pigments, as well as gilding, were employed for their decoration. Observe the excellence of the modelling in the feet of some of the smaller figures. Of the heads and hands belonging to these statues several were found amid the charred débris of the chapels. One of these heads. $13\frac{1}{4}''$ high, of the conventionalised type, belonging probably to one of the standing figures in chapel $N^{17}$, is illustrated in Pl. VI*a*.

Retracing our steps and turning westward past stūpa $N^5$ we come to the little stūpa $N^7$, which is built on the ruins of an older monument. In its relic chamber, which was constructed of neat kañjūr stones, was found the crystal lion illustrated in Pl. XVI, 11; and, beneath it a casket of Gandhāra stone, containing a small box of silvery bronze with some minute bone relics within, accompanied by two small pearls and one bead of bright blue paste. STŪPA $N^7$.

In the narrow space between $P^7$ and $P^{10}$ was a broken Gandhāra sculpture representing the offering of honey by the monkey to the Buddha, and a little below it was a small earthen pot containing five gold coins of the later Kushān period, one solid gold ear-ring with pearls attached to it, a few gold beads, plain and fluted, and a broken ornament of beaten gold with a granulated border. This deposit seems to have been placed here after the adjacent buildings had become buried in débris.

BUILDINGS $P^1$ AND $P^2$.

A little to the west of this point the visitor passes through a narrow passage between the buildings $P^1$ and $P^2$. The former of these was a stūpa of the Kushān period, the latter a chapel in the later style of masonry. In this passage are two colossal Buddhas side by side, seated on a stone plinth. Their hands rest in the lap in the attitude of meditation (*dhyāna-mudrā*), but their heads, unfortunately, are missing.

TANK.

In the open space into which we now emerge is a tank with four small stūpas on its northern and eastern sides, which are of some interest in connexion with the much disputed question of Kushān chronology. The tank is built of a rough variety of masonry coated with lime plaster, and on its north side is a flight of steps leading to the bottom. Now, the foundations of the Stūpas $K^2$ and $K^3$ project well over the northern end of the steps, and the tank, therefore, must have fallen into disuse and been filled in before ever the stūpas in question were built. But, as the tank itself was not built until the first century A.D. during the Scytho-Parthian epoch, it follows that the stūpas can hardly be assigned to a date earlier than the 2nd century, though they may be considerably more modern than that. In the stūpa $K^3$, however, was found a relic-vase containing ashes and three coins of Kanishka, and in the stūpa $P^6$, which is apparently contemporary with it, was another earthen

STŪPAS $K^3$ AND $P^6$.

vase and ten coins of Huvishka and Vāsudeva, five of which were found inside the vase along with some ashes, and five outside. This is one of the links in a long chain of evidence at Taxila which proves that the Kushans followed and did not antedate the Parthians.

STŪPA K[1].

On the west side of the tank the Stūpa K[1] is also worthy of notice. Observe in particular the seated image of the Buddha in the niche on the northern side, and also the cornice and other details of a distinctively Hellenistic character.

On to the north side of this stūpa were subsequently built several small chambers, probably chapels, facing north. They stand on a common base adorned with a row of stunted pilasters alternating with niches of the same design as those above the terrace of the Main Stūpa, namely, trefoil arches and doorways with sloping jambs in which figures of the Buddha were placed.

VIEW OF THE SITE AND THE SURROUNDING COUNTRY.

From this point it is well worth while to ascend the higher ground to the north and take a bird's-eye view of the whole site and of the surrounding country (Pl. IX). Five years ago the ground level of the whole excavated area was little lower than this elevated plateau, and standing on the edge of the latter we get a good idea of the amount of débris that had to be shifted before this array of buildings could be exposed to view. The point to which this débris rose around the Great Stūpa itself is still clearly visible on the sides of the structure.

As to the character of the remains that still lie buried beneath the plateau on which we are standing, a clear indication is afforded by other Buddhist sites in the neighbourhood. If the visitor will look at the other eminences in the valley, he will see that many of them are crowned by groups of ancient ruins, and he will observe that in each group there is a circular mound standing side by side with a square one. In each of these cases the circular mound covers the remains of a Buddhist stūpa, and the square one adjoining it the remains of a monastery. Similarly, at the Dharmarājikā Stūpa, which was the chief monument of its kind at Taxila, it may be taken for granted that quarters were provided for the monks in close proximity to the sacred edifice, and it is obvious from the configuration of the ground that these quarters must have occupied the northern part of the site. To this monastery no doubt belong the high and massive walls which have been laid bare on the eastern side of the plateau, but judging by the results obtained from other trial trenches it is doubtful if this area would repay excavation.

BUILDING H[1]. Descending again to the lower level we pass, on our right hand, the shrine H[1] which was probably intended for an image of the Dying Buddha. This building exhibits three types of masonry, representing three different periods of construction. In the original shrine the stonework is of the small diaper pattern, but subsequently this shrine was strengthened and enlarged by the addition of a contiguous wall in the larger diaper style, as well as of a second wall enclosing a *pradakshiṇa* passage and portico in front. Later on, when the level had risen several feet, additions in semi-ashlar masonry were made, and other repairs were carried out at a still later date. The only minor antiquities of interest in this building were

28 debased silver coins of the Greek king Zoilus (Pl. III, 14). They were brought to light beneath the foundation of the earliest chapel, where they appear to have been deposited before the site was occupied by the Buddhists.

The two small pits $M^4$ are of interest only as affording some evidence as to the age when the Gandhāra School of Art was flourishing. They were used for the mixing of lime stucco and their floors were composed of Gandhāra reliefs laid face downwards. As the reliefs in question were already in a sadly worn and damaged condition before they were let into the floor, it may safely be inferred that a considerable period—say a century or more—had elapsed between the time when they were carved and the construction of the pits. But from the character of their walls the latter appear to have been constructed in the 3rd or 4th century A.D. and it follows, therefore, that the reliefs cannot be assigned to a later date than the 2nd or 3rd century A.D. Evidence of a precisely similar character was also obtained from the chamber $B^{17}$ on the eastern side of the Great Stūpa. Two pits $M^4$.

The complex of chambers $G^1$ to $G^8$ comprises chapels erected at different periods and in different styles of masonry. From an architectural point of view they are in no way remarkable, but the chapel $G^5$ merits notice, because it was here that one of the most interesting relics yet discovered in India was unearthed. The find was made near the back wall of the chapel opposite the Main Stūpa and about a foot below the original floor. It consisted of a steatite vessel with a silver vase inside, and in the vase an inscribed scroll and a small gold casket containing Chapels $G^{1-8}$.

some minute bone relics. A heavy stone placed over the deposit had, unfortunately, been crushed down by the fall of the roof, and had broken both the steatite vessel and the silver vase, but had left the gold casket uninjured, and had chipped only a few fragments from the edge of the scroll, nearly all of which were fortunately recovered (Pl. VII). The inscription, which is in the Kharoshṭhī character and dated in the year 136 (circa 78 A.D.), records that the relics were those of the Lord Buḍdha himself. It reads as follows:—

**Inscription of the year 136.**

L. 1. *Sa* 100. 20. 10. 4. 1. 1. *Ayasa Ashaḍasa masasa divase* 10. 4. 1., *iśa divase pradistavita Bhagavato dhatu*[*o*] *Ura*[*sa*]—

L. 2. *kena Ḷotaphria-putrana Bahaliena Noachae nagare vastavena tena ime pradistavita Bhagavato dhatuo Dhamara*—

L. 3. *ie Tachhaśie Tanuvae Bodhisatvagahami maharajasa rajatirajasa devaputrasa Khushanasa arogadachhinae*

L. 4. *sarva-buddhana puyae prachaga-budhana puyae araha*[*ta**]*na puyae sarvasa* [*tva**] *na puyae mata-pitu puyae mitra-macha-ñati-sa*—

L. 5. *lohi*[*ta**]*na puyae atmano arogadachhinae nianae hotu* [*a*]. *de samaparichago*.

"In the year 136 of Azes, on the 15th day of the month of Āshāḍha, on this day relics of the Holy One (Buddha) were enshrined by Urasakes(?), son of Lotaphria, a man of Balkh, resident at the town of Noacha. By him these relics of the Holy One were enshrined in the Bodhisattva chapel at the *Dharmarājikā stūpa* in the district of Tanuva at Takshaśilā, for the bestowal

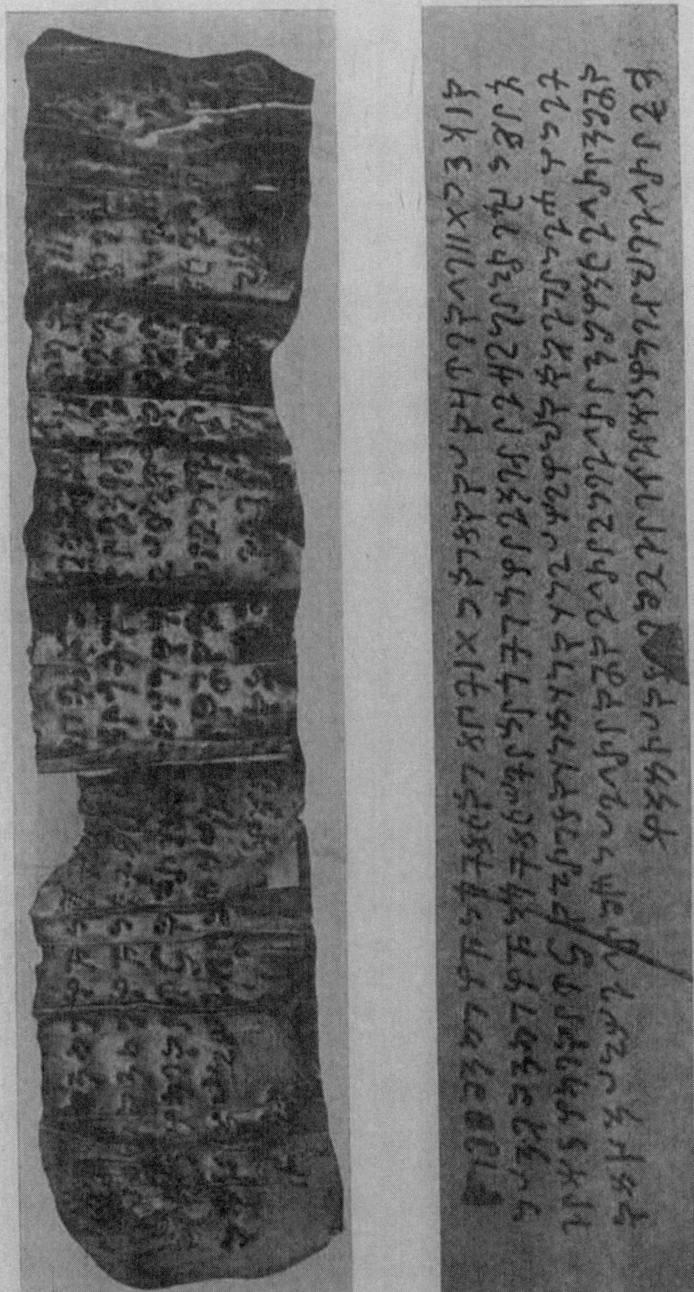

DHARMARAJIKA STUPA: SILVER SCROLL INSCRIPTION AND TRANSCRIPT.

of perfect health upon the great king, king of kings, the divine Kushana; for the veneration of all Buddhas; for the veneration of the private Buddhas; for the veneration of arhats; for the veneration of all sentient beings; for the veneration of (his) parents; for the veneration of (his) friends, advisers, kinsmen, and blood-relations, for the bestowal of perfect health upon himself. May this gift be........".[1]

In the chamber $G^4$, on the highest floor level, were numerous kañjūr blocks belonging to a small stūpa. These blocks were scattered in a heap on the floor defying any attempt to reconstruct from them the design of the stūpa from which they had fallen. In one of the blocks were found two relic caskets of steatite. One of the caskets contained a smaller one of ivory, and in the latter was a still smaller one of gold adorned with rough geometric and floral designs. Inside this gold casket were a piece of calcined bone, a small gold bead, and a number of small pearls of various sizes and shapes. In the other casket, which was shaped like a Greek pyxis, was a smaller silver box roughly ornamented and containing a smaller golden casket with some thin gold leaf and two pieces of calcined bone inside.

It was in this block of buildings that there was also found, besides other antiquities, the bearded male head of terracotta figured in Pl. VI *d*, the style of which differs markedly from the conventional style of the early mediæval period.

[1] This inscription was published by the writer in *J. R. A. S.*, October 1914, pp. 973-86.

CHAPEL R[1]. The small circular stūpa R[4] was, as I have stated above, repaired and enlarged on several occasions. The first addition made to the original structure was a square base of neatly cut kañjūr blocks adorned with slender pilasters of the Corinthian order and a simple dentil cornice. Then came the two small square projections on the western face of this base; and at the same time a shallow portico or chapel was formed against this western face by running out two short walls from the north-west and south-west corners of the stūpa. Lastly, this portico or chapel was enlarged to about double its size by a further addition on the west. Now, the projections are built in a type of masonry which can be assigned with some degree of certainty to the second century of our era. But contemporary with them are the very interesting stucco reliefs with which they and the western face of the stūpa base are adorned. That these sculptures belong to the Gandhāra School of Art, a glance at them will suffice to show; and we thus obtain here another useful link in the chain of evidence which determines the age when this school was flourishing. Observe the reliefs in the small recesses between the projections and side walls. One of them—on the south face of the south projections—portrays the departure of Gautama from Kapilavastu, accompanied, as usual in the Gandhāra School, by the *vajra*-bearer. The other —on the northern face of the northern projection— portrays the horse Kaṇṭhaka taking leave of his master. The animal is kneeling to kiss the feet of Gautama, while Chhandaka and another figure on the one side, and the *vajra*-bearer on the other, look on.

Besides these reliefs, numerous stucco and terracotta heads were found in the débris which had accumulated in and around this chapel.

BUILDING L.

The building L, which stands immediately to the south of R[1], was a double-chambered chapel standing on a high plinth, access to which was provided by a flight of steps on the northern side. All that is now left of it are the plinth walls constructed of large diaper masonry of the Kushān period, but round about the building were found numbers of Gandhāra stone sculptures which had served to decorate the superstructure and which, there can be no doubt, were contemporary with it and therefore of the Kushān period. Two specimens of these carvings are illustrated in Pl. VIII. They are as follows :—

(*a*) Relief, 19 in. high, depicting, probably, the presentation of offerings to the Buddha, after his enlightenment. In the centre is Buddha seated cross-legged on a cushioned throne with his right hand raised in the attitude of protection (*abhaya-mudrā*). To his proper right is the *Vajra*-bearer holding the thunderbolt (*vajra*) in his right hand. In front of him are three female worshippers, bearing offerings of flowers or uncertain objects in their hands. To his proper left are four other worshippers, three with offerings, the fourth in an attitude of adoration (Pl. VIII *a*).

(*b*) Damaged relief, 19 in. high, depicting Buddha's first sermon in the Deer Park near Benares. In the centre is Buddha seated crossed-legged on throne beneath a canopy of foliage and turning with his right hand the Wheel of the Law (*dharma-chakra*[1]), which is supported by a *triratna*[2] set on a low pedestal. On either side of the pedestal is a horned deer to symbolise the Deer Park. On the right and left of the Buddha, a Bodhisattva. Behind, on right, the *Vajrapāṇi* holding fly-whisk (*chaurī*) in right hand and *vajra* in left. In front of him, two ascetics seated, and above, a heavenly musician (*gandharva*) flying (Pl. VIII *b*).

In spite of the large number of Gandhāra sculptures recovered, the inscribed records on them are rare and fragmentary. The most interesting is one engraved in Kharoshṭhī letters on the side of a stone lamp, which speaks of the "Agradharmarājikā stūpa" at Takshaśilā.

APSIDAL TEMPLE I[3].

On the western side of the site the most striking edifice in old days must have been the apsidal temple or 'Chaitya Hall,' where the faithful came together for their devotions. It dates from Kushān times and is built of large diaper masonry similar to that used in building L. In plan, the temple is generally similar to the 'Chaitya Halls' excavated in the hill-sides at Kārlī, Ajaṇṭā, Ellora and other places in Western and Central India, but in this case the interior of the apse is octagonal instead of round. Inside the apse are the remains of an octagonal stūpa of kañjūr stone, 2 ft. 6 in. below the base of which is a floor

[1] *Dharma-chakra*='Wheel of the Law'. The technical expression for Buddha's first sermon in the Deer Park (*Mṛigadāva*) near Benares is *Dharma-chakra-pravartana*, which literally means "the turning of the wheel of the law." Hence the symbol of the first sermon became a wheel, which is sometimes set on a throne and sometimes on a column.

[2] See p. 41, note 1.

PLATE VIII.

DHARMARAJIKA STUPA.

(a) OFFERINGS TO BUDDHA AFTER HIS ENLIGHTMENT.

(b) THE FIRST SERMON.

which must have been laid before the apsidal temple was built. From what remains of the nave, it appears to have consisted of nothing more than a passage corresponding in width with one side of the octagon and flanked by very thick walls on either side. The temple is of special interest as being one of the very few structural buildings of the kind known to exist in India, and the first to be discovered in Northern India. Since its excavation, however, another and far more imposing example has been found in the city of Sirkap (p. 81).

**Chapels E and F[1].**

The last of the structures which we shall notice on this site is the range of small chapel cells (E and F[1]) on the western edge of the plateau. The cells are raised on a plinth about 4 feet high and ascended by flights of steps on their eastern side. In two of them, namely: E[1] and E[2], are the solid foundations of circular stūpas descending to a depth of 10 ft. below the plinth level and evidently intended for the support of a heavy superstructure. A similar stūpa with its superstructure still intact has been found in one of the cells of the monastery at Mohṛā Morādu (p. 108).

In another of the chambers, F[1], was a floor of glass tiles of bright azure blue with a few other colours—black, white and yellow—mixed with them. These tiles average $10\frac{1}{4}$ in. square by $1\frac{1}{8}$ in. thick and are of transparent glass, the first complete specimens of their kind which have yet come to light in India. In connexion with these tiles it is interesting to recall the Chinese tradition that glass making was introduced into China from Northern India. The tiles were found laid in a somewhat careless manner on a bed of earth, and it was evident that they were not occupying the position for which they were originally intended. Probably they had been brought from the procession path of the Great Stūpa (p. 38).

From the Dharmarājikā Stūpa our way lies northwards through a defile in the Hathiāl ridge and thence across the fields and up a steep hill-side to the Kunāla stūpa. The distance is about a mile and a quarter, and the track is rough and stony.

PLATE IX.

VIEW OF THE DHARMARAJIKA STUPA FROM NORTH.

## CHAPTER V

### Stūpa of Kunāla

At the time when Hsüan Tsang visited Taxila, the city of Sirkap had been deserted for more than five centuries and its ramparts and buildings must long have been in ruins. The city in which the pilgrim himself sojourned, is the city now known as Sirsukh, where numerous structures of the early mediæval period are still traceable. In the neighbourhood of this city there were four famous Buddhist monuments which the pilgrim described. One of these was the tank of Elāpatra, the Dragon King; another was a stūpa which marked the spot where, according to the Buddha's prediction, one of the four Great Treasures will be revealed when Maitreya appears as Buddha[1]; a third was the stūpa of the "sacrificed head," said to have been built by Aśoka and situated at a distance of 12 or 13 *li* to the north of the capital; the fourth was a stūpa also said to have been built by Aśoka to commemorate the spot where his son Kunāla had had his eyes put out. The first and second of these monu-

Identification of the Stūpa.

[1] The four Great Treasures referred to are those of Elāpatra in Gandhāra, Pāṇḍuka in Mithilā, Piṅgala in Kaliṅga, and Saṅka in the Kāśi (Benares) country. *Cf.* T. Watters, *On Yuan Chwang*, p. 243.

ments were rightly identified many years ago by General Cunningham: the one with the sacred tank now known as the Pañjā Sāhib at Hasan Abdāl, the other with a ruined stūpa which crowns the ridge above Baotī Piṇḍ. As to the other two, Cunningham laboured under the false idea that the city which Hsüan Tsang visited was the city on the Bhiṛ mound instead of in Sirsukh, and he could not, therefore, but fail to identify the location of the two stūpas. Now that we know that the earliest city of Taxila was on the Bhiṛ mound and the latest in Sirsukh, it is clear that the stūpa of the "sacrificed head" is none other than the Bhallaṛ Stūpa, which occupies a commanding position on the extreme western spur of the *Sarḍa* hill, and it is probable that the memorial of Kunāla's misfortune is the stūpa which occupies a hardly inferior position on the northern slopes of Hathiāl, commanding a splendid view of the lower city of Sirkap and of the whole of the Haro valley (Pl. X). Hsüan Tsang describes this stūpa as being above 100 ft. high, and situated to the south-east of the city of Takshaśilā on the north side of the south hill. The blind, he says, came here to pray, and many had their prayers answered by the restoration of their sight.[1] He then proceeds to narrate the story of Kunāla: of how his stepmother Tishyarakshitā fell in love with him and induced Aśoka to send him as Viceroy to Takshaśilā; of how she then wrote a despatch in her husband's name and sealed it with the seal of his teeth while he slept, bringing accusations against Kunāla and ordering his eyes to be put out; of how the minis-

[1] *Cf.* T. Watters, *On Yuan Chwang*, Vol. I, pp. 245 *sq.*

PLATE X.

VIEW OF THE KUNALA STUPA FROM N.-W.

ters shrank from executing the order, but the prince himself insisted on obedience to his father; of how he then wandered forth with his wife and begged his way to the far-off capital of his father; of how his father recognised him by his voice and the strains of his lute; and of how the cruel and vindictive queen was put to death and the prince's eye-sight restored at Bodh-Gayā through the help of the Buddhist Arhat Ghosha.[1]

The southern hill referred to by Hsüan Tsang can only be the hill of Hathiāl which bounds the Haro valley on the south; and the most conspicuous stūpa on its northern side is the one on the northernmost ridge erected almost directly over the remains of the old wall of Sirkap. This stūpa rests on a lofty rectangular base which measures 63 ft. 9 in. from east to west by 105 ft. 1 in. from north to south and was provided with a stepped approach at its northern end. The base rises in three terraces, the lowermost DESCRIPTION.

[1] In its essence the story of Kunāla and Tishyarakshitā is the same as that of Hippolytus and Phaedra, and it is not unlikely that it was derived from the classical Greek legend. Such legends must have been familiar enough among the Eurasian Greeks in the north-west of India. Witness, for example, the drama of Antigone portrayed on a vase found at Peshāwar. Some versions of the story represent Aśoka as sending his son to restore order in Takshaśilā on the advice of a Minister of State, not through the instrumentality of Tishyarakshitā, and in some versions the prince dies after his return home without any miracle transpiring to restore his eye-sight. His real name was Dharmavivardhana and his father called him Kunāla because his eyes were small and beautiful, like those of the Himavat bird of that name. The blinding of the prince was the outcome of evil *karma* wrought in a previous existence. According to one story, he had blinded 500 deer; according to another, an arhat; or, according to the Avadānakalpalatā, he had taken the eyes (relics) out of a *chaitya*. Ghosha, the name of the arhat who restored his eye-sight to Kunāla, was also the name of a famous oculist of this district. *Cf*. T. Watters, *loc. cit.*

of which is relieved by a series of stunted Corinthian pilasters resting on an elaborated "torus and scotia" moulding and formerly surmounted by a dentil cornice and copings, with Hindu brackets of the "notched" variety intervening between the capitals and the cornice. The middle terrace is plain, but covered with a coating of plaster. The uppermost terrace was decorated in much the same way as the lowest one, but was nearly three times as high; and the base mouldings and entablature were proportionately more massive and elaborate.

Of the superstructure of this monument only a fragment of the core has survived *in situ*, but the form and construction of the terraced base, coupled with the style of the decorative details, leave no room for doubt that the Kunāla Stūpa is of the same age as the great Bhallaṛ Stūpa on the opposite side of the valley; and to judge by the character of the many architectural members belonging to the upper part of the structure which were lying in considerable numbers round its base, it seems fairly safe to conclude that the elevation of the drum and dome resembled that of the Bhallaṛ Stūpa; in other words, that the drum was circular and strikingly lofty in proportion to the size of the monument and that it was divided into six or seven tiers, slightly receding one above the other, which were adorned with rows of pilasters, friezes and dentil cornices in much the same fashion as the terraces of the base. As in the Bhallaṛ Stūpa, too, as well as in other stūpas of this date, the relic chamber was no doubt placed near the top of the edifice; for no trace of any chamber was found in or below the plinth of the building.

A remarkable feature of this monument is the delicate concave curvature of the plinth. The western side of the stūpa, for example, measured in a straight line from end to end, is 74 ft. 10 in. long; but the line thus drawn does not coincide with the actual line of the plinth, which recedes gradually inwards towards the centre, the greatest distance between the arc and the chord being three inches. It is well known, of course, that entasis of the columns and curvature of other lines, horizontal as well as perpendicular, was systematically employed in Greek architecture in order to correct the apparent defects caused by optical illusions; and it may be that the idea was introduced from Western Asia, along with the many other Hellenistic features which characterise the architecture of Taxila and the North-West. But, if this was so, it would appear that the optical principles which underlay the idea could not have been properly understood by the builders of the Kunāla Stūpa; for in this case the concave curvature has the effect of exaggerating the illusion, instead of correcting it.

This stūpa, which I assign to the third or fourth century A.D., was not the earliest monument to be erected on this interesting site. Buried in the core of the structure and towards its north-west corner, was found another and very much smaller stūpa which appears from its style to have been erected in the first century A.D., at a time when the city wall alongside of it on the east was still standing intact. This older edifice is perched on a small rocky eminence and is standing to a height of 9 ft. 8 in. It is constructed of rough blocks of limestone and consists of a square plinth with drum and dome above, the only feature that has disappeared being the crowning umbrella. Originally the rough masonry was covered with lime plaster on which the mouldings and other decorative details were worked, but all the plaster has now fallen from the sides.

MONASTERY. Immediately to the west of the Kunāla Stūpa and at a slightly higher level is a spacious and solidly built monastery in the semi-ashlar style, which is manifestly contemporary with the later stūpa. It is standing to a height of between 13 and 14 feet and consists, apparently, of two courts—the larger to the north and the smaller to the south, the total length of the exterior wall opposite the stūpa being about 192 feet, and the width of the larger court about 155 feet. The larger court is of the usual form (*chatuḥśāla*) with an open rectangle in the centre surrounded by a raised verandah and cells. In the cells are small arched niches for the reception of lamps. Only the east side of this monastery has yet been excavated and even on this side the digging has not yet been carried down to the floor level of the cells.

## CHAPTER VI

### SIRKAP

Before descending into the lower city of Sirkap we shall halt for a moment at the fortifications on the eastern side of the city, a short section of which has recently been excavated. These fortifications are constructed of rubble masonry throughout, like other structures of the Greek and Scytho-Parthian epochs, and vary in thickness from 15 ft. to 21 ft. 6 in. They are strengthened at intervals by solid bastions, which, so far as they have been examined, are rectangular in plan. In some cases the bastions are further supported by sloping buttresses which were apparently added at a later date. The height of the walls and bastions was probably between 20 and 30 feet, and it may be assumed that the bastions were built in two storeys, of which the upper was doubtless hollow and loopholed. The walls between the bastions would also be loopholed above and provided with a terrace on the inner side for the use of the defenders. CITY WALL.

As stated in the first chapter (p. 4), the city of Sirkap appears to have been founded during the supremacy of the Indo-Greeks in the second century B.C. and to have remained in occupation during the Scytho-

Parthian and Kushān epochs until the reign of Wima-Kadphises. Of the buildings hitherto excavated inside its walls those in the uppermost stratum appertain mainly to the Early Kushān and Parthian settlements. Below them is a stratum of remains which are assignable probably to the Scythian epoch, and below these, again, two more strata belonging to the Greek era, after which virgin soil is reached at a depth of between 14 and 17 feet. Of the pre-Parthian remains our information, as yet, is relatively meagre, since the digging has been chiefly confined to the remains nearest the surface, the object in view being to obtain as clear an idea as possible of the lay-out of the city in Parthian and Kushān days before opening up the structures beneath, and thereby not only confusing the plan but possibly jeopardising the safety of the buildings.

From the bird's-eye view of the excavations which he got from the stūpa of Kunāla, the visitor will have observed that they extend in a broad strip from the northern wall right through the heart of the lower city, and that they comprise a long section of the High Street running due north and south together with several large blocks of buildings on either side of it. Among these buildings is a spacious Apsidal Temple of the Buddhists and several small shrines belonging either to the Jaina or to the Buddhist faith ; but most of them are dwelling houses or shops of the citizens, and one, distinguished from the rest by its size and by the massiveness of its construction, is almost certainly a

PALACE. palace. This last named building is at the south end of the excavations and the first to be reached after leaving the Kunāla Stūpa. It stood almost at the corner, where the two streets from the North and West Gates must have met, and thus occupied a commanding position in the lower city. On the western side, which faces the High Street, it has a frontage of 352 feet, and from west to east it measures 250 feet, but its eastern limits have not yet been reached. The oldest parts of the palace are constructed of a rough rubble masonry and date probably from the Scytho-Parthian era, but there are numerous later repairs and apparently several additions, particularly in the Zenana apartments on the north, though they cannot always be distinguished with precision. In courts of special importance, as for instance in the large court marked $C^{12}$, an ashlar facing of kañjūr stone is also employed, while some of the thresholds consist of blocks of limestone. In many of the courts and rooms chases indicate that beams were let into the walls and wooden panelling probably affixed thereto. In other chambers the surface of the walls was covered with lime or mud plaster, no doubt finished with a coating of paint.

So far as it has been exposed, the palace consists of five series of apartments arranged in groups around a central court. The plan of these can best be appreciated by standing on the wall in the middle of the Palace at the point marked × in the plan (Pl. XI). The large court in the centre of the west side, together with the chambers round about it, contained the chief living rooms, one of which ($B^{16}$) is a bathroom with a small tank in the middle and a channel to carry off the water. This court is paved with irregular blocks of limestone and on its southern side is a raised daïs with a frontage of 27 ft. 10 in. and a depth of 20 ft. 5 in. This probably was the court of private audience (Dīwān-i-Khāṣṣ). To the south of this court is a smaller court ($C^{16}$) with chambers round about, which probably served for the retainers and guard. On the opposite or north side of the main court is another large group of chambers which were the zenana quarters of the women, separated from the rest of the palace by substantial walls. Beyond them, again, to the north are other chambers which appear to have been added later. On the east side of the palace are two more groups of apartments. The group on the south consists of a spacious court with chambers on the west and a raised daïs, which no doubt supported an open hall, on the south. This court seems to have been used for semi-official or public purposes (Dīwān-i-Āmm), the rooms around it doing duty as offices. Leading off from it on its north side is another complex of rooms which probably served as reception rooms for guests. The rooms in this court are less regularly built and somewhat smaller than in the rest of the palace.

Although this palace is considerably larger and built more substantially than the private houses, there is nothing at all pretentious in its planning or sumptuous in its adornment. This is a feature which is specially commented on by Philostratus, the biographer of Apollonius, who says, when speaking of the palace, that they saw no magnificent architecture there, and that the men's chambers and the porticoes and the whole of the vestibule were very chaste in

PLATE XI.

SIRKAP: PLAN OF PALACE.

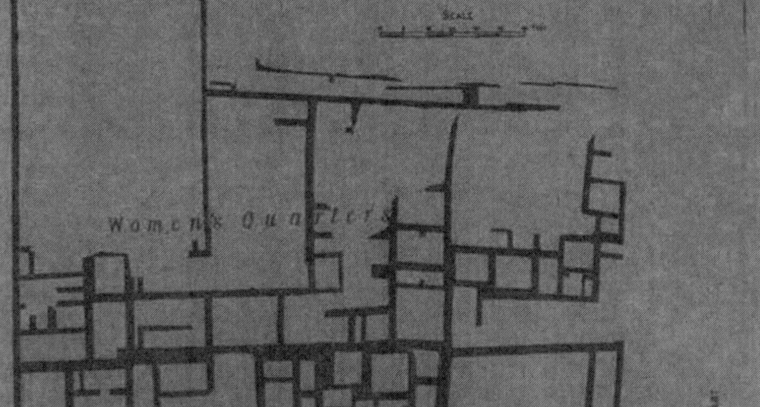

style.[1] These remarks of Philostratus are valuable as affording another proof of the substantial correctness of his account of Taxila, which, as we shall presently see,[2] finds somewhat remarkable corroboration in the peculiar character of the private houses.

In spite, however, of the palace being so bare and unadorned, its remains are singularly interesting, if only for the sake of the plan they disclose—the first plan of a building of this kind which has yet been recovered in India; and this interest is still further increased when we realise that, so far as it has been exposed, the plan bears a striking resemblance to those of the Assyrian palaces of Mesopotamia. This will best be understood by comparing it with the palace, for example, of Sargon at Khorsabad.[3] In the latter we have the same great court surrounded by chambers, and on the one side of it, the same court for retainers; on the other, the apartments of the zenana. Here, also, we have the other half of the palace occupied, just as it is at Taxila, by reception and public rooms. In the palace of Sargon there is another block of apartments farther out on this side, at the point where some more chambers are also beginning to appear in the palace at Taxila. The Zikurrat tower, which in the palace of Sargon was placed at the side of the zenana, is a feature which appertains peculiarly to the Assyrian religion. Whether it will be found in the Taxila Palace, remains to be seen. Possibly it may prove, as the excavation advances, that its place was taken by

[1] Philostratus, *op. cit.* Bk. II, Ch. XXV.
[2] P. 71.
[3] Perrot and Chipiez, *Histoire de l'Art antique*, Tome II, Pl. V.

some other sacred edifice. That a palace at Taxila of the Greek, Śaka or Pahlava period should have been planned on the same lines as an Assyrian palace of Mesopotamia need occasion no surprise, when we bear in mind the vitality and persistency of the influence which Assyria exerted upon Persia, Bactria and the neighbouring countries. But it certainly gives an added interest to these buildings and helps us in our efforts to disentangle the archæological problems of this period.

The small antiquities found in this palace consist of terracottas and potteries, various small bronze, copper and iron objects, beads, gems and coins. Among the last mentioned was a deposit of 61 copper coins of Azes I, Azes II and Aśpavarma, Gondopharnes, Hermaeus and Kadphises I. One find of special interest that deserves to be mentioned here, was a number of earthenware moulds for casting coins, which were found in a room or shop just outside the palace and near its south-west corner. The coins, of which the impress is clear in many of the moulds, are those of Azes II. Probably the moulds belonged to the plant of some forger of the Pahlava epoch. Eight of them are complete and twenty broken.

**Plan of Houses.** Proceeding from the palace down the High Street in the direction of the North Gate of the city, we come to several large blocks of dwellings, separated one from the other by narrow side streets.[1] Although

[1] It will be noticed that both streets and houses rise higher and higher as they recede from the High Street. The reason of this is that the High Street was kept clear of débris, while the débris on either side of it was steadily accumulating.

the plans of these houses exhibit considerable variety, they were all based on the same principles. The unit of their design, that is to say, is the open quadrangle surrounded by chambers (*chatuḥśāla*), just as it is in the palace described above, and this unit is repeated two, three, four or more times according to the amount of accommodation required by the occupants, the small rooms fronting on to the street being usually reserved for shops. The walls are constructed either of rough rubble or of the diaper masonry which came into fashion at the beginning of the Kushân period; and both inner and outer faces were covered with lime and mud plaster, to which traces of paint are still found adhering. Wood was used for the fittings, such as doors and windows, as well as for roof timbers, and in some cases, apparently, for panelling on the walls. The fact that no tiles have been found in any of these houses indicates that the roofs were flat and covered with mud. A remarkable feature of these houses is that, although in some cases there are doors communicating between two or more rooms, there are no doors giving direct access from these rooms to the interior court or to the streets outside—the practice having apparently been to enter these lower chambers by means of stairways or ladders descending from the rooms above. This practice is alluded to by Philostratus, who says that the houses are so constructed that, if you look at them from the outside, they appear to have only one storey, but, if you go into them, you find in reality that they have underground rooms the depth of which is equal to the height of the chambers above.[1] As a matter of fact, the lower floor of the houses is not actually underground, but anyone seeing only a single row of windows from the street, and having to descend from the upper chambers into the *tahkhānās* below, which were unprovided with doors or windows, might well be excused for calling them underground cellars.

Another noticeable feature of the Sirkap dwellings is the amount of accommodation provided in them, which, even if they were not more than two storeys, was greater than a single family in that age would be ikely to require. It may be that, like the "insulae" of ancient Rome or the blocks of tenements in many Italian and other cities of to-day, they were occupied by several families together; but it is also a plausible hypothesis that this quarter of the city was the University[2] quarter, and that these were the houses of the professors and their pupils, who would certainly need more accommodation than could be obtained in any ordinary dwelling.

Of the stūpas referred to there are two typical examples—both probably of Jaina origin.[3] The one in block G—the first block to which we come on the right (east) side of the High Street—stands in a courtyard facing the street and consists of a small rectan-

SHRINE IN BLOCK G.

[1] Philostratus, *Life of Apollonius of Tyana*, Bk. II, Ch. XXIII.

[2] The Fame of Taxila as a University city belongs to an earlier age, *viz.*, the age of the Jātakas, but it is not unreasonable to assume that it still continued a seat of learning up to the first century of our era.

[3] The reason for regarding these stūpas as of Jaina rather than Buddhist origin, is that they closely resemble certain Jaina stūpas depicted in reliefs from Mathurā.

gular base adorned with a series of five pilasters on each side, with a simple base moulding, and with a cornice relieved by the familiar "bead and reel" pattern. The drum, dome and umbrella of this stūpa have fallen, but parts of them were unearthed in the débris of the courtyard, along with portions of two Persepolitan columns with crowning lions[1] which used to stand, probably, on the corners of the base, and numerous members of the balustrade which ran around its edge. In the centre of the base and at a depth of about 4 feet from its top was a small relic chamber, and within this chamber was a steatite casket containing eight copper coins of the Scythian king Azes I, and a smaller casket of gold, in which were some fragments of calcined bone, small pieces of gold leaf, and cornelian and agate beads. Azes I came to the throne about the year 58 B.C., and this stūpa probably dates, therefore, from the latter part of that century.

Close by the south side of the staircase is a small square plinth, the purpose of which is doubtful. A plinth of a similar kind occurs at the shrine in block G and at the bigger stūpa at Jaṇḍiāl. Judging from their superficial character, it seems hardly likely that they were intended to sustain the weight of a column. They may, perhaps, have served as the bases of lampstands.

**SHRINE OF THE DOUBLE HEADED EAGLE IN BLOCK F.**

The stūpa in the next block (F), which belongs to the same period, is a somewhat more pretentious building (Pl. XII). On the front façade of the building

[1] Imitated no doubt from the pillars which the Emperor Aśoka set up at many of the most famous Buddhist stūpas.

all the pilasters are of the Corinthian order, two having rounded and the remainder flat shafts. The interspaces between these pilasters are relieved by niches of three varieties. The two nearest the steps resemble the pedimental fronts of Greek buildings; those in the centre are surmounted by ogee arches like the familiar "Bengal" roofs; and those at the corner take the forms of early Indian *toraṇas*, of which many examples are portrayed on the sculptures of Mathurā.[1] Perched above each of the central and outer niches is a bird, apparently an eagle, and it will be observed that one of these eagles is double-headed. The presence of this motif at Taxila is interesting. It is known to occur for the first time in Hittite sculptures from Western Asia; and it is found also on an early ivory of the Geometric period from Sparta. But later on it seems to have been especially associated with the Scythians, and we may well believe that it was the Scythians who introduced it at Taxila. From the Scythians, probably, it was adopted into the Imperial Arms of Russia and Germany, and from Taxila it found its way to Vijayanagar and Ceylon.

The whole facing of kañjūr stone, including mouldings and other decorations, was originally finished with a thin coat of fine stucco and, as time went on, numerous other coats were added, several of which, when first excavated, showed traces of red, crimson and yellow paint. Both drum and dome were probably adorned with decorations executed in stucco and painted, and the dome was surmounted by three

[1] *Cf.* V. A. Smith, *Jain Stūpa and other Antiquities of Mathura*, Pl. XII.

PLATE XII.

SIRKAP: VIEW OF SHRINE OF THE DOUBLE HEADED EAGLE.

umbrellas. At the edge of the steps and round the base of the stūpa was a low wall decorated on the outside with the usual Buddhist railing, parts of which were found in the courtyard below. A good idea of the appearance of the stūpa, when intact, may be obtained from a relief of the Mathurā School published in V. A. Smith's *Jain Stūpa* and *other Antiquities of Mathura,* Pl. XII, which appears to have been executed at no great length of time after the erection of this building. But in this relief the style of the stūpa is more pronouncedly Indian than the stūpa in Sirkap. In the latter, the whole basis of the decorative design is Hellenistic, the mouldings, pilasters, dentil cornice and pedimental niches being all classical, while the only Indian features are such subsidiary details as the *toraṇa,* the ogee-arched niche and the brackets above the pilasters. It remains to add that the chamber containing the relics in this stūpa was found in the centre of the base at a depth of 3 ft. 2 in. below its top, but it had long since been rifled of its contents.

In the block of buildings (F) to which this shrine belongs a discovery of considerable value was made in the shape of an Aramaic inscription carved on what appears to have been an octagonal pillar of white marble (Pl. XIII*a*). This inscription was found built into the wall between two chambers, $a^1$ and $a^2$, in the north-west corner of the block, and, inasmuch as these chambers date approximately from the reign of Azes I, it must have been buried in its present worn and broken condition before the beginning of the Christian era. The letters as well as the language are Aramaic and of a type which is to be assigned to the fourth

ARAMAIC INSCRIPTION.

century B.C. but the meaning of the record is still a matter of uncertainty. Dr. L. D. Barnet and Prof. Cowley interpret it as referring to the erection of a palace of "cedar and ivory,"[1] but according to another interpretation it relates to a private compact and the penalty to be paid for breaking it. The discovery of this inscription is of special interest in connexion with the origin of the Kharoshṭhī alphabet, since it confirms the view that Kharoshṭhī was derived at Taxila (which was the chief city of the Kharoshṭhī district) from Aramaic, the latter having been introduced into the North-West of India by the Achaemenids after their conquest of the country about 500 B.C.

MINOR ANTIQUITIES OF SIRKAP.

The minor antiquities recovered from these and other houses in Sirkap are many and various. They include large collections of earthenware vessels of numerous shapes and sizes, from lamps and drinking goblets and incense burners up to the great store-jars, three to four feet in height, in which grain, oil and the like were kept; terracotta figurines and toys; stone bowls, goblets, decorated plaques and dishes; iron vessels and utensils, among which are folding chairs, tripod stands, horse's bridles, keys, sickles, spades, swords, daggers, shield bosses and arrow-heads; bronze and copper cups, lamps, caskets, scent bottles, ornamental pins, bells, finger rings; several thousands of coins and numerous pieces of gold and silver jewellery. A description of these many classes of antiquities is beyond the scope of this guide book,

JEWELLERY FROM HOUSE E.

but there are two finds of gold and silver jewellery

[1] *J. R. A. S.* 1915, pp. 340-7.

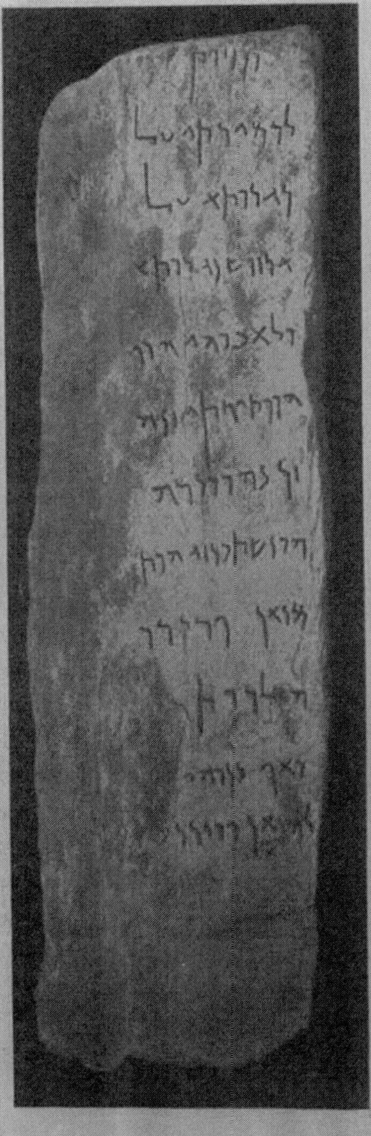

(a) SIRKAP: ARAMAIC INSCRIPTION.

(b) JAULIAN: STUPA CASKET.

SIRKAP: PLAN OF HOUSE E AND APSIDAL TEMPLE D

PLATE XIV.

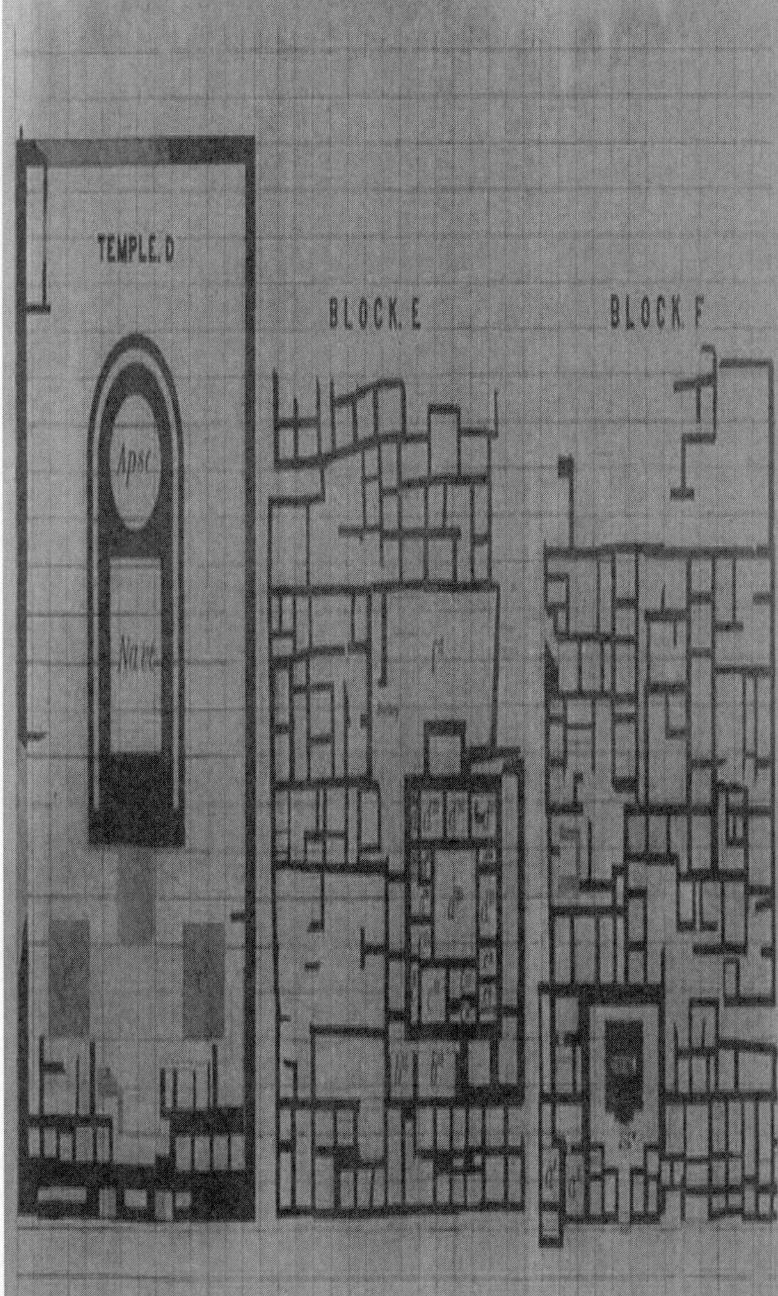

which deserve particular mention, both because of their intrinsic value and interest, and because the objects comprised in them have been removed to Lahore, where many visitors to Taxila may not perhaps have an opportunity of seeing them. Both finds were made in Block E, the one in chamber $C^{18}$ in the second or Scytho-Parthian stratum and the other at a slightly higher level on the north side of the central courtyard (Pl. XIV). The objects recovered were as follows :—

FROM CHAMBER $C^{18}$.

Bronze statuette of the child-god Harpocrates, holding a finger to his lips in token of silence. In the left hand he carried some object, possibly a flower, which has disappeared. Late Hellenistic work (Pl. XV).

About two feet below this statuette in the same chamber was brought to light an earthen jar closed at the top with a disc and containing the objects enumerated below. The disc is composed of two thin plates, iron on the inside, silver on the outside, rivetted at the edge with silver nails. Originally, it may have done duty as the boss of a shield.

Head of Dionysus in silver repoussé, with stand beneath.[1] The head of the god is bald on top and wreathed with a grape-vine. His ears are pointed. In his right hand he holds a two-handled wine-cup (*cantharus*). Behind the head passes the curved staff (*thyrsus*) with a bell suspended at its end. The front

[1] The stand is not illustrated in Pl. I.

of the stand is adorned with a conventional palmette and rosette; behind it, is a curved projection which enabled the head to be set in a slanting position on the table. The relief is Hellenistic in style and of very high class workmanship (Frontispiece).

3. Silver spoon, with handle terminating in a cloven hoof and attached to the back of the spoon by a "rat-tail" ridge. Greek pattern. Precisely similar spoons have been found at Pompeii (Pl. XVI, 15).

4. Two pairs of gold bangles. The ends were closed with separate discs of beaten gold.

5. Pair of gold ear-rings, provided with clasp attached by ring hinge. The clasp is of a double horse-shoe design ornamented with cinquefoil rosettes, two hearts and strap. The hearts and rosettes were formerly inlaid with paste, which has now perished (Pl. XVI, 1 and 2).

6. Two ear-pendants of gold. They are composed of rings decorated on the outside with double rows of beads and granules, with granulated bud-like drops depending from them (Pl. XVI, 3 and 5).

7. Flower-shaped pendant of gold, composed of six petals, backed by granulated ribbings and six smaller heart-shaped petals at their base, one inlaid with paste or jewels. Attached to the lips of the larger leaves is a ring with granulated edge, from which chains were suspended with bells at their ends (Pl. XVI, 4).

8. Plain gold finger ring, with flattened bezel engraved with Kharoshṭhī legend, "*Sadaralasa* (?)" and Nandipada symbol (Pl. XVI, 6).

9. Gold hoop finger ring, with oval bezel enclosing

PLATE XV.

SIRKAP: FIGURE OF HARPOCRATES.

Plate XVI.

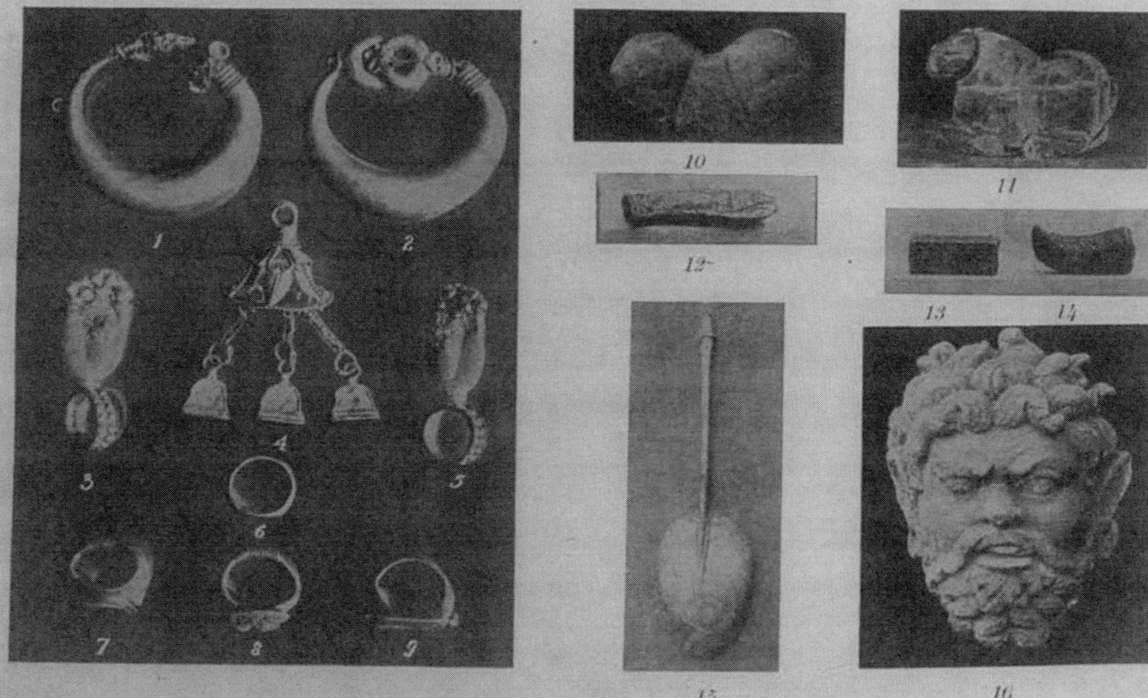


SIRKAP: JEWELLERY FROM HOUSE E AND OTHER OBJECTS.

cornelian engraved with cornucopia, fluted vase, and spear in the Hellenistic style (Pl. XVI, 7).

10. Gold hoop finger ring, with oval bezel enclosing silver inlay. The device on the silver is too corroded to be distinguished (Pl. XVI, 8).

11. Gold hoop finger ring, with flat rectangular bezel and clusters of four drops on either side. The inlaid stone is lapis-lazuli, engraved with the figure of a warrior armed with spear and shield and an early Brāhmī inscription to his proper left. The style of the engraving is Hellenistic. The inscription reads :—. . . . *samanavasa* (Pl. XVI, 9).

12. Gold chain, composed of four double plaits, fitted with ring at one end and hook at the other (Pl. XVII, 8).

13. Six cylindrical pendants belonging to necklace. The casing is gold open-work of various reticulated designs, enclosing cores of turquoise paste, green jasper, and other stones. Attached to each are two small rings for suspension (Pl. XVII, 7).

14. Seven open-work gold beads, probably inlaid with paste (Pl. XVII, 6).

15. Pair of gold ear-rings, bound with wire at ends (Pl. XVII, 4 and 5).

16. Gold ear-ring of coarse workmanship (Pl. XVII, 3).

17. Oval locket of gold. The jewel is missing from the centre.

18. Pair of diamond-shaped attachments, probably for ear-rings, of gold inlaid with garnets *en cabuchon* (Pl. XVII, 9).

19. Pair of hollow club-shaped gold pendants (Pl. XVII, 10).

20. 60 hollow gold beads, round and of varying sizes (Pl. XVII, 13).

The articles contained in the above deposit appear to have been buried during the 1st century B.C. But a number of these articles had then been in use for a considerable time, as is proved by the extent to which they had been worn. I assign the bronze statuette to the 1st century B.C. and the lapiz-lazuli ring and the head of Dionysus, which is certainly the finest example of Greek work yet discovered in India, to the previous century.

From the north side of Central Courtyard.

21. Gold repoussé figure of winged Aphrodite or Psyche (Pl. XVII, 11).

22. Round gold repoussé medallion. In centre, winged Cupid dancing, encircled by flowing lines. This and the previous figure are of coarse workmanship, made apparently by beating a thin gold plate into a mould (Pl. XVII, 12).

23. Nine oval-shaped jacinths cut *en cabuchon* and hollowed behind. They are engraved with various intaglio figures of victory, Eros, busts, etc.

24. One flat cornelian ditto, with bust intaglio. Broken.

25. Three garnets *en cabuchon*, dot and comma shape, used for inlay.

26. Two oval glass gems—(*a*) with flat face banded in green, white and blue; engraving indistinct; (*b*)

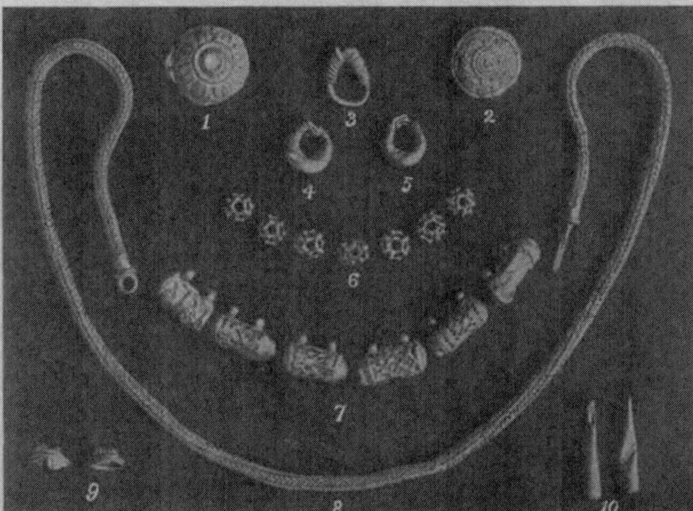


*a*

*b*

*SIRKAP: JEWELLERY.*

*en cabuchon*, of dull brown glass; engraving indistinct. Fractured.

27. 74 pieces of gold necklace. Each piece is hollow and pierced laterally for two strings (Pl. XVII, 14).

28. Pieces of turquoise paste and crystal cut *en cabuchon* and flat, in various designs. These as well as the gems enumerated above, appear to have been used for inlaying.

29. 21 silver coins of new types belonging to the Parthian kings, Sasan, Sapedanes, and Satavastra and the Kushān king, Kadphises II (?).

In the block of buildings opposite to E, on the western side of the High Street, a noteworthy feature is the stūpa at the south-east corner, access to which is provided on the east side by a double flight of seven steps faced with squared kañjūr masonry. The plinth of this stūpa is composed of thick walls of stone radiating from the middle with the interspaces between them filled with débris. A pit sunk in the centre of this core revealed a square chamber at a depth of between seven and eight feet below the surface; but, unfortunately, the chamber had been broken into and rifled in days long gone by.

The next building on the east side of the High Street is the Great Apsidal Temple of the Buddhists to which I referred on p. 57. This temple, the plan of which will be apparent from Plate XIV, faces to the west. It stands in a spacious rectangular courtyard with two raised platforms to right and left of the entrance of the temple and rows of chambers for the monks against the west compound wall. The temple

**Apsidal Temple D.**

was built on the ruins of earlier buildings of the Scytho-Parthian epoch, and with a view to providing a level court and at the same time adding to the impressiveness of the building, these earlier structures were filled in with débris and a raised terrace was thus created, access to which was provided by two flights of steps on the street front. The platforms to the right and left ($C^1$ and $C^2$) as one enters the court, are the foundations of two small stūpas, amid the fallen masonry of which were found numerous stucco and terracotta heads and other decorative objects which had once served to adorn the edifices. One of them, a stucco head of a Greek Satyr with pointed ears, is illustrated in Pl. XVI, 16.

The value of these terracottas and stuccos is all the greater because their date can be fixed with approximate certainty. In the débris of the courtyard both here and at other spots numerous coins were unearthed belonging mainly to Kujūla-Kadphises and Hermæus, with a few of earlier date mingled with them. From these it may be inferred that the building was already falling to decay in the latter part of the 1st century A.D.

In the middle of the court stands the great Apsidal Temple, and just as the court is raised above the level of the street, so the temple itself is raised on a plinth well above the level of the court. It consists of a spacious nave[1] with a porch in front and a circular

[1] Gen. Cunningham found in the nave the remains of some colossal figures of burnt clay. The apse he took to be a circular well or underground room, distinct from the temple. *Cf. C.S.R.*, 1863-4, pp. 127-8.

apse behind, the whole surrounded by an ambulatory passage (*pradakshiṇā*), to which access was gained from the front porch. The plan, in fact, is generally similar to that of the Sudāma cave in the Barābar hills,[1] but in the latter case there was no porch in front and no passage around the outside of the chambers. In the middle of the apse, which measures 29 feet in diameter, there must originally have been a stūpa, but treasure-seekers of some bygone age had utterly destroyed it.

The exceptional depth (22 ft.) of the foundations of the apse is explained partly by the excessive weight of the superstructure, partly by the fact that they had to be carried through the loose débris of earlier structures, until virgin soil was reached.

Near the old floor level is a curious horizontal break in the masonry of the walls, which is now filled with earth. This break marks the position where timbering, which has since decayed, was originally inserted in the stone work.

As to the elevation of this temple, it is impossible to speak with certainty, but it may plausibly be surmised that the *pradakshiṇā* passage was lit by windows pierced in its outer walls, as was the case with the temple at Jaṇḍiāl to be described presently, and that light into the nave and apse was admitted through the western doorway or a window above it. The roof appears to have been of wood covered with earth, as is indicated by the remains of timber and a large number of iron nails, bolts, clamps, etc., found in the débris.

[1] *Cf.* Fergusson, *Indian and Eastern Architecture,* Vol. I, p. 130.

**Stūpa Court A.** Of the buildings between the Apsidal Temple and the northern wall of the City, there is none that calls for particular notice except the large court with a square stūpa in its centre on the east side of the High Street. This court differs from those previously described both in being more spacious and in having a number of living cells disposed around its four sides. Possibly it was intended rather for public, and the others rather for private worship. The stūpa in the centre had been despoiled of its relics; but the relic chamber still contained, among other objects, some broken pieces of what must once have been a singularly beautiful crystal casket, the fine workmanship of which suggests that it dates from the Maurya age. From the fragments remaining it is evident that the casket, when intact, would have been too large to go inside the relic chamber; and it must be inferred, therefore, that it was enshrined there in its present broken condition. The probability is that the relics deposited here were taken from some much older monument and that the crystal casket in which they had reposed having been broken, the fragments of it were scrupulously preserved. That contact with the relics would invest such fragments with a special sanctity is clear from the story of the Brahman Droṇa, who at the division of the relics of the Buddha, received as his share the casket in which the Mallas had placed them; and it is proved also by the discovery of similar fragments in stūpas at Sañchī, Sārnāth and elsewhere.

**City Gate.** When their excavation is complete, the north gate of Sirkap and the adjoining fortifications will probably afford as much interest as anything in the city, especially as this is the only example of a city gateway of the early period that has yet been brought to light in India. At present, the digging is not sufficiently advanced to make the disposition of the defences entirely clear, but it already seems evident that the main gateway must have been masked on its outer side by a barbican, and that the barbican was pierced by a second gateway set at right angles to the main one. To the west of the gate and against the inner face of the wall is a range of substantially built rooms, which we may assume to have been occupied by the guard, and on the opposite side of the High Street are the remains of one of the ramps by which the defenders could mount on to the wall. Immediately inside, as well as outside, the gateways the gradient must always have been a steep one, and, as the level of the ground inside the city rose, it became steeper and steeper, necessitating the construction of a deep drain to carry off the rush of water. During the latest period of the city's occupation this northern entrance appears to have been closed, and the remains of various later walls and apparently of stūpas also, can be seen in the actual gateway.

## CHAPTER VII

### Jaṇḍiāl

**Temple.** From Sirkap we now proceed due northwards through the suburbs known as "Kachchā koṭ" to the two lofty mounds in Jaṇḍiāl, between which the ancient road to Hasan Abdāl and Peshāwar probably ran. The mound to the east of the road, which then rose to a height of some 45 feet above the surrounding fields, was superficially examined by Gen. Cunningham in 1863-64, and at a depth of 7 or 8 feet below the surface he discovered some walls of a large building which he surmised to be an ancient temple. Curiously enough, the General was quite correct in believing that an ancient temple lay concealed in this mound, but the walls which he himself unearthed belonged to a comparatively late structure of the mediæval epoch. The ancient temple which has now been laid bare was found at a depth of 8 or 9 feet still lower down.

The position of this temple is a very commanding one, standing as it does on an artificial mound some 25 feet above the surrounding country and facing the north gate of the city of Sirkap. Its length, including the projection in front of the portico to the back wall, is 158 feet, and excluding the peristyle, a

PLATE XVIII.

JANDIAL TEMPLE: PLAN.

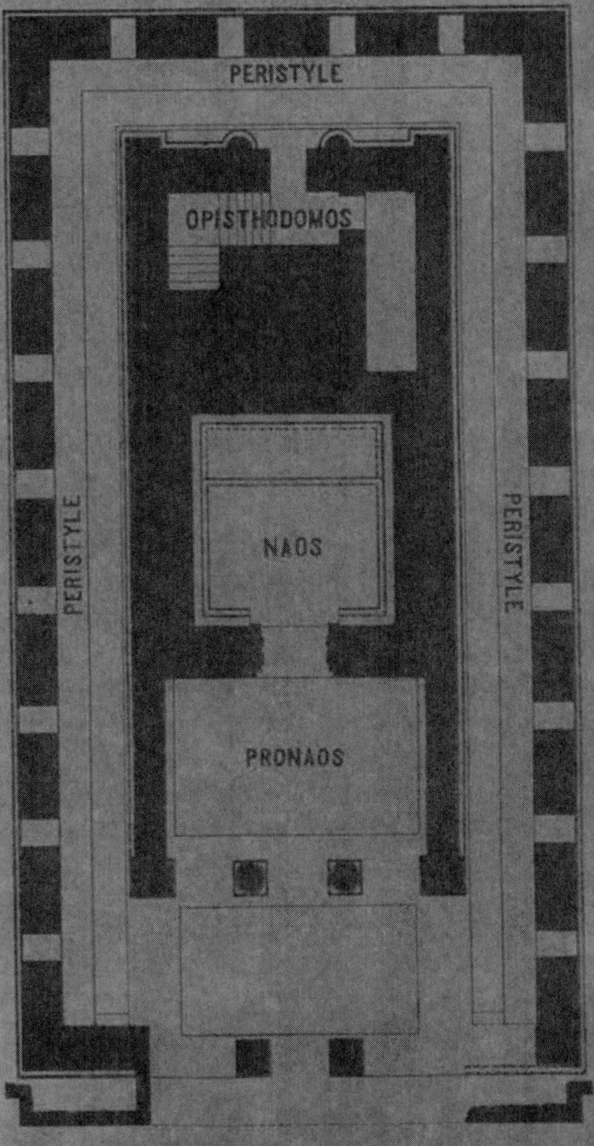

little over 100 feet. Its plan is unlike that of any temple yet known in India, but its resemblance to the classical temples of Greece is striking (Pl. XVIII). The ordinary Greek peripteral temple is surrounded on all sides by a peristyle of columns and contains a *pronaos* or front porch, a *naos* or sanctuary, and, at the rear, an *opisthodomos* or back porch, known to the Romans as the *posticum.* In some temples, such as the Parthenon at Athens or the Temple of Artemis at Ephesus, there is an extra chamber between the sanctuary and the back porch, which in the case of the Parthenon was called the "Parthenon" or chamber of the virgin goddess Athene. In the newly excavated temple at Jaṇḍiāl the plan is almost identically the same. In place of the usual peristyle of columns is a wall pierced at frequent intervals by large windows which admitted ample light to the interior, but at the main or southern entrance of the temple are two Ionic columns *in antis, i.e.,* between pilasters, which received the ends of the architrave passing above them. Corresponding to them on the further side of a spacious vestibule is another pair of similar columns *in antis.* Then comes, just as in Greek temples, the *pronaos* leading through a broad doorway to the *naos,* while at the back of the temple is another chamber corresponding to the *opisthodomos.* The only essential difference in plan between this and a Greek temple is that, instead of an extra chamber between the *opisthodomos* and the sanctuary, we have at Jaṇḍiāl a solid mass of masonry, the foundations of which are carried down over 20 feet below the floor of the temple. From the depth of these foundations it may safely be concluded that this mass of masonry was intended to carry a heavy superstructure, which, apparently, rose in the form of a tower to a height considerably greater than that of the rest of the temple. Access to this tower was provided by flights of broad steps ascending from the *opisthodomos* at the rear of the temple and laid parallel with the sides of the edifice. Two of these flights still exist, and it may be assumed that there were at least three more flights above them, probably narrowing in width as they ascended above the roof of the main building. The altitude of this tower may be surmised to have been about 40 feet.

The masonry of the temple is mainly of limestone and kañjūr, originally faced with plaster, patches of which are still adhering to the walls at various points.

The Ionic columns and pilasters, however, are composed of massive blocks of sandstone, the bases, shafts and capitals being built up in separate drums fixed together with square dowels let in the centre, as was also the practice in Greek buildings (Pl. XIX). In the construction of columns in Greek temples it is well known that a fine joint was obtained by grinding down each drum in its bed. In the case of the Jaṇḍiāl temple the same process seems to have been followed, the beds of the drums being roughly chiselled at the centre and a raised draft left at the edge, which was afterwards ground down. The base mouldings of these columns are not very subtle in their outline, but their capitals with their "leaf and dart" and "reel and bead"

Plate XIX.

VIEW OF JANDIAL TEMPLE.

mouldings are of quite a pleasing form. In several of the column and pilaster bases fractures were caused in ancient days, probably by earthquakes, and these fractures were repaired by cutting back the broken stones to a straight edge and dowelling on a separate piece by means of iron pins.

The wall mouldings in the *naos* or sanctum extend round the foot of all four walls, and it is obvious from their existence along the north wall that originally this wall stood free down to its base. At a subsequent date, however, a platform about 3 ft. 6 in. high, was added on this side of the chamber. The door leading from the *pronaos* to the *naos* appears to have been of wood bound with iron, of which many fragments were found in the charred débris strewn over the floor.

As to the superstructure of this temple, the architrave, frieze and cornice were of wood and, no doubt, of the Ionic order, in keeping with the Ionic character of the columns, pilasters, and bold mouldings around the base of the walls. Of wood, too, was the roof construction; but the roof could not have been of the ridge type usual in Greek temples. Had the roof been sloping, tiles must have been used on the outside, and some of them must inevitably have been found among the fallen débris. But there was not a trace of anything on the floor of the temple, except the great charred beams of wood, long iron nails, door hinges, and a thick layer of clay mixed with masses of plaster from the walls and charcoal. It may be concluded, therefore, that, save for the tower in the middle of the building, the roof of the temple was flat, like the roofs of most oriental buildings, and composed of half a dozen inches of earth laid over the timbers.

To what faith this unique temple was dedicated, we can only surmise. That it was not Buddhist, seems patent from the total absence of any Buddhist images or other relics among its débris, as well as from its unusual plan, which is unlike that of any Buddhist chapel that we know of. For similar reasons, also, we must rule out the idea that it was Brahmanical or Jaina. On the other hand, the lofty tower in the middle of the building and immediately behind the sanctum is very significant. My own view is that this tower was a *zikurrat*, tapering like a pyramid, and ascended in just the same way as the *zikurrats* of Mesopotamia; and I infer from its presence, as well as from the entire absence of images, that the temple belonged to the Zoroastrian religion. On the summit of the tower the faithful would offer their prayers in praise of the Sun, Moon and all else which led their thoughts to Nature's God; and in the inner sanctuary would stand the sacred fire altar with the daïs at the side from which the priests would feed it.[1] We know that the idea of the Assyrian *zikurrat* was familiar to the Persians, and there is nothing more likely than that they borrowed its design for their fire temples. Indeed, the *zikurrat* tower at Firuzabad has been thought by

[1] *Cf.* Dr. J. J. Modi in the *Times of India*, Aug. 12, 1915. I myself previously took the view that the fire altar was placed on the summit of the *zikurrat*; for we know that in Achæmenian times the Persians set their fire altars in high places and raised on lofty substructures. But Dr. Modi, the eminent Parsi scholar, doubts whether, amid the cosmopolitan surroundings of Taxila, the fire altar could thus have been exposed to view.

many authorities actually to be a fire altar. Moreover, in favour of my hypothesis, it must be remembered that this temple was constructed in the Scytho-Parthian epoch, at a time when Zoroastrianism must certainly have had a strong foothold at Taxila.

It is possible that this is the temple described by Philostratus in his *Life of Apollonius*, in which he and his companion Damis awaited the permission of the king to enter the city. "They saw", he says, "a temple in front of the wall, about 100 feet in length and built of shell-like stone. And in it was a shrine which, considering that the temple was so large and provided with a peristyle, was disproportionately small, but nevertheless worthy of admiration; for nailed to each of its walls were brazen tablets on which were portrayed the deeds of Porus and Alexander." The words "in front of the wall" define the position of the Jaṇḍiāl temple accurately, and the travellers coming from the north, would naturally wait outside the north gate of the city. The description, too, of the inner sanctum as disproportionately small is significant; for this is a specially noticeable feature of the Jaṇḍiāl Temple. On the other hand, the temple is considerably more than 100 ft. in length, unless we exclude the peristyle. The words λίθου κογχυλιάτου I take to mean, not "*of porphyry*", as they are translated by Conybeare and other editors, but "*of stone covered with stucco,*" shell having been used in India from time immemorial for the making of stucco.

**Stūpas and Monastery in Mound B.**

On the second of the two mounds, which lies a little to the west of the one just described, was another building also of massive proportions and of about the same age as the Zoroastrian Temple; but here the superstructure has entirely vanished and there remains nothing but a complex of foundation walls. Further north, at a distance of about 400 yards from the Temple were two more low mounds, designated A and B, respectively, in the map (Pl. XXIX). In the latter, which lies to the east of the former, have been unearthed the remains of a medium-sized stūpa set in the square courtyard of a monastery. The stūpa is of two periods, having originally been built in the Scytho-Parthian epoch, and rebuilt probably in the third century of our era. The earlier structure is now standing to a height of only a little over 2 ft. above the old floor level. It is square in plan, with a projecting staircase on its southern face, and a spacious relic chamber in the centre. Round the base runs a moulding of the usual pattern, and above is a series of square pilasters, six on each side of the building, which were once surmounted by a dentil cornice. Near the foot of the steps on the eastern side is a square plinth, similar to those by the side of the shrine in block G in Sirkap.

When this stūpa and the monastic quarters connected with it had fallen to decay, another stūpa and a second series of cells were erected on a different plan above their ruins. This later stūpa has a circular plinth and is constructed of limestone blocks in the semi-ashlar style.

This monument was partly excavated some years ago by Sir Alexander Cunningham, who appears to have penetrated as far as the later circular structure only, which he describes as being 40 feet in diameter and which he erroneously identifies with the stūpa erected by Aśoka on the spot where Buddha had made an offering of his head (p. 116). Prior to Cunningham's excavation the relic chamber had been opened by the villager Nur, who, without being aware of the fact, seems to have thrown out the relics concealed within; for in the spoil earth which he had left at the side of the stūpa, I found a small silver casket lenticular in shape, containing a smaller one of the same pattern in gold, and in the latter a small fragment of bone. The larger vase in which these caskets had no doubt reposed, had disappeared.

The second and smaller mound, which lies within a hundred feet of stūpa B, is also mentioned by Sir Alexander Cunningham as having been opened by the villagers and as containing a small ruined "temple." In reality it is a stūpa of almost precisely the same type as the earlier of the two just described, though the masonry and ornamental details are somewhat inferior. No relics were found in this stūpa, nor did the débris yield any minor antiquities of interest. STŪPA A.

## CHAPTER VIII

### SIRSUKH, LĀLCHAK AND BĀDALPUR

POSITION OF SIRSUKH.

To reach the city of Sirsukh we must now retrace our steps by way of the Zoroastrian Temple and proceed for about a mile and a half along the main road to Khānpur. Sirsukh, as already stated,[1] is the most modern of the three cities of Taxila, having been founded by the Kushāns, probably during the reign of the great Emperor Kanishka. The mounds which cover the ruins of its southern and eastern ramparts, are still clearly visible from the road alongside the little Luṇḍī nālā, but the northern and western walls have almost entirely vanished beneath the level of the fields or been destroyed, and on these two sides it is only with difficulty that their line can now be traced.

SIRSUKH FORTIFICATIONS.

Of the eastern fortifications a short section has been exposed to view near the south-east corner of the city, and it is these excavations which will be our first objective. The wall, which is constructed of rough rubble faced with neatly fitting limestone masonry of the large diaper type, is 18 ft. 6 in. in thickness, and is provided at the base both on its inner and outer face with a heavy roll plinth, which was added after

[1] P. 6 *ante*

the wall itself had been completed, in order apparently to strengthen its foundations. On the outer face of the wall, and separated from each other by intervals of about 90 feet, are semi-circular bastions, access to the interior of which is provided by a narrow passage carried through the thickness of the wall. Both the bastions and the wall itself are furnished with loopholes, which are placed immediately above the plinth referred to, at a height of rather less than five feet above the old floor level. In the case of the bastions, these loopholes widen towards the outside and are closed on the outer face of the wall with triangular arches which give them a singularly western appearance. Beneath them, in the interior of the bastions, is a hollow horizontal chase in the wall, now filled with earth, which marks where timbers were once let into the masonry. Still lower down (on a level, that is to say, with the old floor and opposite the entrance of the bastions) there is, in some of them, an aperture which no doubt served the purpose of a drain. The floors of the bastions were composed of lime concrete containing a large admixture of river sand.

If we compare these fortifications with those of Sirkap, we shall find that they differ from the latter in several essential features. In the first place, they are faced with the large diaper masonry characteristic of the early Kushān period instead of the rubble masonry characteristic of the Greek and Scythian periods. Secondly, they are pierced with loopholes for the use of defenders standing on the ground floor. Thirdly, the bastions are semi-circular in plan instead of rectangular, and are hollow within instead of solid. In the case both of Sirkap and of Sirsukh it may be assumed that the bastions were divided, like the bastions of later Indian fortresses, into two or more storeys, and that the upper storeys were hollow like the lowest storey at Sirsukh. In both cases, too, it may be taken for granted that the wall was provided with an upper terrace and with lines of loopholes corresponding with the terrace, from which the defenders could shoot down on an attacking force.

Two other striking features in which the city of Sirsukh differs from its predecessor, are its almost rectangular plan and its situation in the open valley, its builders having manifestly placed more reliance on their artificial defences than on any natural advantages which the hills might afford them. Whether these new features were the outcome of developments in military engineering in India itself, or whether they were introduced by the foreign invaders, the Kushāns, from Central Asia or elsewhere, is a question which we have not yet enough data, either monumental or literary, for determining.

The minor finds from the bastions of Sirsukh include copper coins of Hermæus and Kadphises I, which were recovered on the floor level, an ivory mirror handle and a deposit of 59 copper coins of Akbar the Great, which were unearthed near the surface.

TOFKIĀN. In the interior of Sirsukh conditions are less favourable for digging than in Sirkap; for, on the one hand, nearly all the area enclosed within the walls is low-lying and abundantly irrigated, with the result that the ancient remains are buried deeper beneath the alluvial soil than in Sirkap; on the other hand, the few mounds which rise here and there among the cultivated fields and which doubtless mark the sites of relatively important structures, are now occupied by graves and ziārats or modern villages, such as those of Piṇḍ Gākhṛā and Piṇḍorā, and, while any disturbance of the graves or ziārats is out of the question, the removal of the modern dwellings could only be effected at an inordinate cost. The only spot inside the city where excavation has been started is between the village of Tofkiāñ[1] and the mound of Piṇḍorā, where dressed stones and pottery had often been turned out by the plough and where there was promise of ancient structures being found relatively near the surface. Here a complex of buildings has been revealed which may eventually prove of considerable interest. It comprises parts of two courts, a larger one to the west and a smaller one to the east, with a series of chambers disposed around them and a connecting passage between. As to the extent and plan of this building, all that can be said at present, is that the principle on which it is designed, namely, the principle of the open court flanked by rows of chambers, is the

[1] *Cf. C. S. R.*, Vol. II, p. 133, and Vol. V, p. 67. Cunningham describes the find in one of the mounds near this village of a copper plate inscription dated in the year 78. But Cunningham himself is in doubt as to whence precisely the inscription came. In one place he says that its findspot is situated nearly a thousand yards to the south-west of Sirsukh, while in another he speaks of its having come from the village of Tofkiāñ inside the city, the reason for these conflicting statements being that the copper plate in question was discovered, not by Cunningham himself, but by a *bhishti,* named Nur, who gave different accounts of it at different times, and whose versions, therefore, are altogether unreliable. The remains which I have so far excavated near the village belong to a much later date than this inscription.

same as that followed in the older structures of Sirkap; and, judging by the dimensions and structural character of what has been exposed, it may be surmised that the whole will prove to be an elaborate and extensive building not unlike the one which I have designated "the palace" in the earlier city. In one respect, however, there is a noticeable difference between these two structures. In contradistinction to the other buildings in that city, the palace of Sirkap is provided with doorways leading from the courtyard to the ground floor chambers, as well as from one chamber to another; here, in Sirsukh, there is no evidence of any such openings in the walls, and we are left to infer that access to the ground floor chambers was provided, as it was provided also in the ordinary houses of Sirkap, by steps descending from the first floor rooms.

It remains to add that the wall stretching across the north side of the court appears to be the foundation of a raised plinth which probably supported a pillared verandah; that the masonry of the walls is semi-ashlar above the ground level, but approximates to rubble below; and that in some of the chambers were found large earthenware jars of the type usually employed for the storage of grain, oil or water, as well as coins of Kadphises II, Kanishka and Vāsudeva and various other minor antiquities.

## Lālchak.

**Buddhist stūpa and monastery.** Between one and two hundred yards from the north-east corner of Sirsukh and on the pathway to the village of Gaṛhī Sayyadān was a group of four small mounds, known locally as Lālchak. These four mounds covered the remains of a Buddhist settlement containing stūpas, shrines and monasteries, which appear to date from about the fourth century A.D. Most striking among them is the small monastery in the northern part of the site (Pl. XX). It is standing to a height of between seven and eight feet above the ground level and contains a vestibule in front, four chambers for habitation leading off from it, and a small apartment on the west side, which probably served as a storeroom. The entrance is in the middle of the southern side and is approached by a flight of four stone steps. A second stairway, also of stone, led from the western end of the vestibule to the upper storey, which has now perished. No doubt the walls of the upper storey were of stone, but to judge by the large quantities of ashes, burnt earth, iron nails, clamps and the like which were found in the débris, the fittings and upper floor must have been of timber, and the roof of the same material with the usual covering of earth. The date which I have assigned above to this monastery, is based upon the style of its masonry; for no minor antiquities to which a definite date can be assigned, were found associated with its foundations or walls. On the other hand, in the débris a few feet below the surface of the mound there came to light four silver coins belonging to the White Huns, which suggest, though they do not prove, that the building had been burnt out and buried from view before the sixth or seventh century of our era. Indeed, it is quite possible that it was not in occupation for more than a few decades; for, though the stairway is worn and smoothed by the passage of many feet, half a century would be quite enough time to account for this.

Among the minor antiquities recovered from this site were an ornamental *triśūla* and rosettes of copper, a bronze finger ring, iron pickaxe and arrow-head, and a necklace of cornelian, garnet, calcedony, crystal, malachite, lapis-lazuli, gold, pearl, and shell beads.

STŪPA I. To the south-east of the monastery just described and about forty yards distant from it is a stūpa standing in the middle of a rectangular compound.[1] It is square in plan with a broad flight of steps on its northern side. The pilasters which adorn the plinth are of the Corinthian order but stunted and decadent, and surmounted, as is usual in later structures, by Hindu brackets.

Inside the court of this stūpa and to the right and left of the entrance were the remains of two small chapels, of which the one to the east comprised a square sanctum for the image with a portico in front, paved with stone slabs. What was left of the other was too fragmentary to be made out with certainty. The design no less than the construction of this and the following building indicates that they were coeval with the neighbouring monastery described above, and it is therefore of interest to record that a pit sunk in the rubble core of this stūpa yielded 140 tokens and coins of various issues, including some of the city of Taxila, others of Antialcidas, Kadphises II, Indo-Sasanian Kings and Sāmantadeva. It is very unlikely that these

[1] This compound as well as the two small chapels mentioned below and Stūpa II, have been covered in again.

PLATE XX.

VIEW OF LALCHAK MONASTERY.

coins, lying haphazard in the earth, were intentionally deposited there when the stūpa was erected. Their presence may be accounted for on the assumption that the débris used for the core of the stūpa was brought from one of the ancient city sites where such coins are found in abundance.

Between Stūpa I and the monastery were the remains of a second stūpa, of which nothing was left standing except its semi-ashlar foundations. Fortunately, the relic-deposit in the centre of these foundations had not been disturbed. The earthenware pot in which it reposed had been broken by the weight of the débris above, but the deposit itself was intact and proved to consist of thirty beads of gold, garnet, ruby, jasper and shell. The relic bone, which had presumably accompanied them, had crumbled to dust. STŪPA II.

## BĀDALPUR.

Of the great stūpa of Bādalpur, near the village of Bhera, there is little that need be said. In its construction, and doubtless also in its design, it resembled the Bhallaṛ and Kunāla stūpas, and must have been one of the most imposing monuments at Taxila; but it has suffered much from the spoliation wrought by treasure seekers in the past, and apart from its massive plinth, which measures over 80 ft. in length by 20 in. height, there is little enough left of its former grandeur. On the north and south sides of the stūpa are two rows of chambers with narrow verandahs in front, which served as chapels for images; and about 70 yds. to the east are the buried remains of a spacious monastery.

The style of the masonry coupled with the finds of coins, which belonged almost exclusively to the Kushān Kings Kanishka, Huvishka and Vāsudeva, betoken the latter half of the third century A.D. as the probable date when these structures were erected.

## CHAPTER IX

### MOHṚĀ MORĀDU, JAULIĀÑ, ETC.

Visitors to Taxila who do not wish to make the round of all the excavations, will find it convenient to omit the remains at Tofkiāñ, Lālchak and Bādalpur, which are of secondary interest only, and to proceed direct from the fortifications of Sirsukh to the two groups of Buddhist buildings at Mohṛā Morādu and Jauliāñ, which in many respects are the best preserved and the most striking monuments of their kind in the North-West of India. The first of these two groups lies about a mile to the south-east of the city of Sirsukh and is situated in a small glen at the back of the village of Mohṛā Morādu. Here, as one goes eastward, the slopes begin to be noticeably greener; for the wild olive and *sonattha* shrub grow freely among the rocks, and the rugged gorge of Meṛi, through which the pathway ascends to the monuments, is singularly picturesque. Inside the glen—or it might better perhaps be termed a cup in the hills—an oblong terrace was constructed by the Buddhist builders, and side by side on this terrace was erected a stūpa and a monastery of commanding size, the former at its western, the latter at its eastern end. When first discovered, both

POSITION OF MOHṚĀ MORĀDU.

monastery and stūpa were buried in a deep accumulation of detritus from the surrounding hills, the only part of the structures visible to the eye being about 5 feet of the ruined dome of the stūpa, which in years gone by had been cut in twain by treasure hunters in search of the relics and, like the Dharmarājikā stūpa, sadly damaged in the process. Beneath this accumulation, however, both buildings proved to be remarkably well preserved, standing actually to a height of between fifteen and twenty feet and still retaining many admirably executed reliefs in stucco on their walls (Pl. XXI).

STŪPA I. In point of architectural design there is nothing specially remarkable about this stūpa, nothing to distinguish it from other memorials of a like character which were erected in the third and fourth centuries of our era. Thanks, however, to its protected position in the hills and other fortunate circumstances, many of the stucco reliefs with which its walls were decorated and which in other cases have almost entirely perished, are here tolerably well preserved; and, though their colouring has mostly disappeared, they suffice to give us a much better idea than we could otherwise have got, of how these monuments looked when they first emerged from the hands of their builders. Apparently, the whole surface of the structure up to the top of the drum was covered with figures; for there are groups of Buddhas and Bodhisattvas, both standing and seated, in the bays between the pilasters (Pl. XXII), and on the face of the pilasters themselves are series of Buddhas ranged one above the other. On the drum, again, above the berm the same figures are repeated

PLATE XXI.

GENERAL VIEW OF MOHRA MORADU MONASTERY.

on a smaller scale, and on each side of the steps was a continuous row of figures disposed in decreasing sizes beneath the raking cornice, just as they might have been in the pedimental groups of a classical temple. In point alike of style and technique the standard attained by the artists who modelled these reliefs is a high one. What strikes one most, perhaps, about the figures and particularly about those in the bays on the south side of the plinth, is their life and movement combined with their dignified composure. This life and movement is specially evident in some of the attendant Bodhisattvas, the swish of whose robes, with the limbs delicately contoured beneath them, is wonderfully true and convincing. Delicate, too, and singularly effective are the hovering figures which emerge from the background to the sides of the Buddhas, as if they were emerging from the clouds. Yet another point that arrests the attention, is the highly successful manner of portraying the folds of the drapery, the technical treatment of which accords with the best Hellenistic traditions and demonstrates most accurate observation on the part of the artists.[1]

Among the many detached heads, found round the base of this stūpa and now preserved in the local museum are several which are in an unusually good state of preservation. Over the surface is a fine slip apparently applied before the final definition was given to the features. The face is left white, but the

[1] In Greek sculpture of the best period the mass of the material was chiselled away and the folds left, as it were, in relief; in Roman and decadent Greek work labour was saved at the expense of truth by merely grooving out the folds from the mass of the material.

lips, edges of nostrils, edges and folds of eye-lids, edge of hair, folds of neck and ear-lobes are picked out in red, and the hair itself is coloured grey black.

STŪPA II. On the south side of the steps of this stūpa is a smaller monument of the same character. It is of the same date and constructed and decorated in much the same manner as the larger edifice, but only a few fragments of the stucco reliefs have survived on the south and west sides.

MONASTERY. The monastery connected with these stūpas is as interesting as the stūpas themselves. In addition to the usual open rectangular court it comprises also several spacious chambers at the eastern side. The entrance to the rectangular court is on the north and is approached by a broad flight of steps with a landing at the top leading into a small portico. On the west wall of the portico is an arched niche containing a remarkably well preserved group of figures in high relief, namely, Buddha in the centre and four attendant worshippers on eithes side.

Passing from the portico into the interior of the monastery we find ourselves in a spacious court with 27 cells ranged on its four sides. In the middle of the court is a depression about two feet deep with steps descending into it on each of its four sides, and at its south-east corner, a square platform which once supported the walls of a chamber. Round about this depression and at intervals of five feet from each other, is a series of stone slabs, the upper surface of which is level with the rest of the court. These slabs acted as bases to the pillars of a broad

PLATE XXII.

MOHRA MORADU: RELIEFS ON STUPA.

verandah which was constructed mainly of wood,[1] and which besides shading the fronts of the ground-floor cells served also to provide communication with the cells on the upper storey. The eaves of the verandah no doubt projected beyond the pillars which supported it, so as to discharge the rain water into the depression in the middle of the court, whence it could be carried off by a covered drain. The height of the lower storey was about twelve feet, as is proved by the ledge and row of socket holes, evidently intended for the timbers of the first floor, in the back walls of the cells on the south side. Access to the upper floor was obtained, not as might have been expected, near the entrance portico, but by way of two flights of steps in one of the cells on the south side of the building. On the western and southern sides of the court all the cells are provided with windows; on the northern side windows were not, perhaps, so necessary, as the light admitted through the cell doors would be brighter; and on the eastern side they were impracticable, inasmuch as there were other chambers at the back of the cells. The windows, placed at a height of about eight feet from the ground, are somewhat narrower at the top than at the bottom, and contract considerably towards the outside. In some of the cells, but not in all, there are small niches, apparently for lamps, like those in the monastery at Lālchak and in the one adjoining the Kunāla stūpa.

The interiors of the cells occupied by the monks were covered, like the rest of the monastery, with a coating of plaster, but were probably destitute of any

[1] The wood construction is evidenced by the mass of charcoal, iron fittings, etc., found in the débris.

decoration. In the verandahs, on the other hand, the wall appears to have been relieved with colours and the wood work was no doubt carved and painted or gilded, while the courtyard was further beautified by effigies of the Buddha of superhuman size set on pedestals in front of the cells, or by groups of sacred figures, in little niches in the walls. Of the larger effigies, remains of seven have survived round about the quadrangle, but only three of these are even tolerably well preserved. In each of these cases there is a particular interest attaching to the smaller reliefs on the front of the pedestals from the fact that they illustrate the dresses worn by lay-worshippers at the time they were set up, namely, in the fourth or fifth century A.D. Of the niches, the best preserved is the one in front of cell 4 on the left side of the monastery, the group in which depicts the Buddha seated in the *dhyāna-mudrā* with attendant figures to the right and left.

A still more valuable discovery than these statues or reliefs, is a stūpa, almost complete in every detail, which was found inside cell No. 9 on the left side of the monastery (Pl. XXIII). It is standing to a height of twelve feet and is circular in plan, its plinth being divided into five tiers, with elephants and Atlantes alternating in the lowest tier, and Buddhas seated in niches alternating with pilasters in the tiers above. The core of the stūpa is of kañjūr, and the mouldings and decorations are of stucco once decorated with colours, *viz.*, crimson, blue and yellow, traces of which are still visible. The umbrella was constructed in sections threaded on to a central shaft of iron, but

MOHRA MORADU MONASTERY: STUPA IN CELL.

in the course of ages this shaft had decayed, and the umbrella was found lying at the side of the stūpa. The edges of the umbrellas are pierced with holes intended apparently for streamers or garlands. This stūpa is, I believe, the most perfect one of its kind yet discovered in Northern India, and as such possesses a very exceptional antiquarian value.

The chambers on the eastern side of the Monastery are reached through a doorway at the back of one of the cells. As originally designed, there were four chambers, the largest of which, to the north, is distinguished by the presence of four kañjūr columns in the centre, and presumably served as the "conference hall" of the community. To what use the other three chambers were intended to be put, there are not yet sufficient data for determining, but it may be surmised that one of them, probably the middle one, was used as a refectory. At a later date—that is, some two centuries after the building of the monastery—this part of it was considerably altered by adding two small closets in the middle chamber and by raising the floor of the chamber in the south-east corner by some eight feet and constructing therein a reservoir, meant apparently for a bath, with a water channel leading down into the middle chamber. The two closets referred to are of unusual form, one being a sort of small *rotunda* with an entrance on its western side, the other rectangular in plan with raised benches on two of its sides. In appearance the *rotunda* looks more like a well than anything else; but its walls are carried down no deeper than the foundations of the monastery, and beneath them there is nothing but solid rock. Possibly this and the other closet adjoining formed part of the baths of the monastery and served as hot and cold chambers.

It remains to add that the original walls of this monastery are in a rather late variety of the large diaper style and may be assigned both on this and other evidence to about the close of the 2nd century A.D. The additions and repairs were in the late semi-ashlar style and were executed, as I have indicated above, about two hundred years later. Many coins of the Kushān kings, Huvishka and Vāsudeva, were discovered on the floor of the monastery. Among other minor antiquities found here was one remarkably fine Gandhāra statue of the Bodhisattva Gautama (?) in almost perfect preservation (Pl. XXIV), several terracotta images of the Buddha which had fallen from the niches in the court, and a massive steatite seal of the Gupta period belonging to one Hariśchandra.

## Jauliāñ.

The other group of Buddhist remains is perched on the top of a hill some 300 feet in height and situated rather less than a mile north-east of Mohṛā Morādu and about half that distance from the village of Jauliāñ. To reach this hill from Mohṛā Morādu the visitor has the choice of two routes: either he may follow the narrow track which leads eastward from the Mohṛā Morādu monastery, or he can retrace his steps as far as the hamlet of Mohṛā Morādu and thence follow the longer path across the fields. In the former case the walk will take about 25, in the latter about 40 minutes.

*MOHRA MORADU MONASTERY: GANDHARA SCULPTURE.*

The monuments in the Jauliāñ group are more highly ornamented and in a still better state of preservation than those at Mohṛā Morādu; for many of them had only just been erected and the rest but newly repaired and redecorated, when they were overtaken by the catastrophe which resulted in their burial. On the other hand, the decorations of these buildings at Jauliāñ is not of so high a quality as those at Mohṛā Morādu. There is less breadth in the treatment of the reliefs, less vitality and movement in the figures, less subtlety in their modelling, and less delicacy in their technique. We shall see presently that there are good reasons for believing that the destruction of the Buddhist settlement at Jauliāñ took place in the fifth century A.D.—at the hands, perhaps, of the invading Huns; and, if this date is correct, then the decorations on the walls of the stūpas can hardly be ascribed to a date earlier than about 400 A.D. The reliefs at Mohṛā Morādu may possibly date from a few decades earlier, but it is probable that the destruction of both these settlements was due to one and the same cause.

**Stūpa Courts.**

Up to the time of writing the position of the original entrance into the stūpa courts has not been definitely ascertained, but we may assume that it was at the south-east corner of the Court. (At present the visitor enters by way of one of the chapels in the north-west corner and finds himself in a large open quadrangle with ranges of small cells intended for cult images along its sides and five moderate sized stūpas, now roofed over for the sake of protection but formerly standing exposed in the open (Pl. XXVI). All these stūpas have lost their domes and cylindrical drums, but their square bases are still adorned with crowds of elaborate stucco reliefs disposed along their walls in horizontal tiers, and are well worthy of attention.) Observe, in particular, the Buddha or Bodhisattva images ensconced in niches with attendants at their sides, and the rows of elephants, lions, or Atlantes in a variety of quaint and distorted postures supporting the superstructure above them; and observe, also, on Stūpa D5 the Kharoshṭhī inscriptions which give the titles of the images and the names of their donors. Kharoshṭhī records of any kind are rare in India, and these are the first that have been found engraved on stucco reliefs.

All the buildings in this lower court were erected at the time when the Main Stūpa was repaired and redecorated in the 4th or 5th century A. D., and it will be noticed that the stonework employed in their construction is the late semi-ashlar variety. The original fabric of the main stūpa itself, which stands in the middle of the upper court, probably dates from Kushān times, but the masonry now visible as well as the stucco decoration dates from two centuries later. On its northern face, a little to the left of the projecting steps, is a seated Buddha figure with a circular hole at the navel and an *ex-voto* inscription in Kharoshṭhī beneath, recording that it was the gift of one Budhamitra, who "delighted in the law" (*dharma*). The hole at the navel was intended for a suppliant to place his finger in when offering prayers against certain bodily ailments. Among the numerous small and richly decorated stūpas which are ranged in rows around the Main Edifice, a special interest attaches to the one

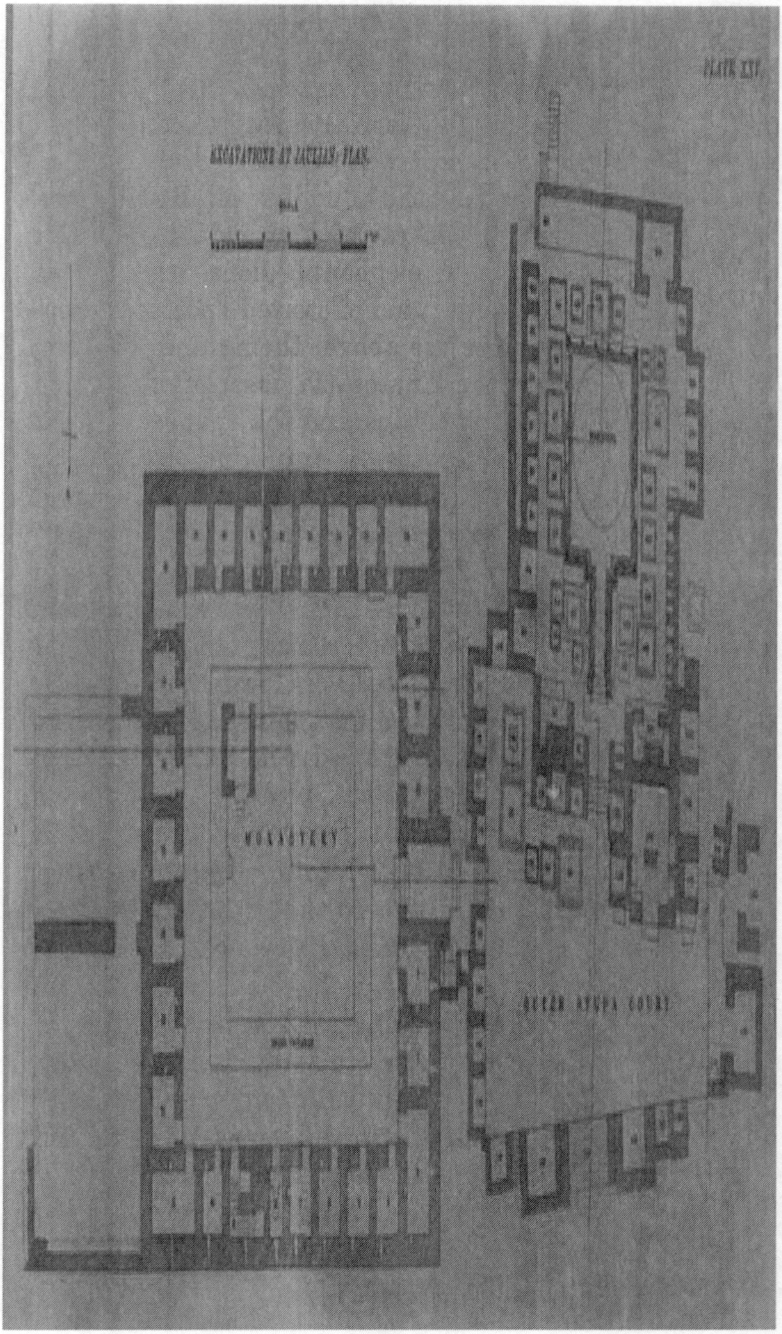
PLATE XXV.
EXCAVATIONS AT JAULIAN: PLAN.
MONASTERY
UPPER STUPA COURT

JAULIAN: GENERAL VIEW

on the south side which is numbered $A^{11}$ in the plan. The relic chamber in this structure was exceptionally tall and narrow, and in it was a miniature stūpa of very remarkable character (Pl. XIII *b*). It stands 3 ft. 8 in. high and is modelled out of hard lime plaster finished with blue and crimson paint and bejewelled round the dome with gems of garnet, carnelian, lapis-lazuli, aquamarine, ruby, agate, amethyst and crystal, cut in numerous shapes and arranged in a variety of simple patterns. The workmanship of this curious relic casket is undeniably coarse and barbaric, but there is a certain quaint charm in its design as well as in the bright and gaudy colouring of the inlaid gems. Down the body of the miniature stūpa runs a hollow shaft, at the bottom of which were the relics themselves, hidden within a smaller copper-gilt receptacle. Another stūpa in the same court which also merits notice, is $A^{15}$ on the west side of the main structure. On it are engraved several more donative inscriptions in Kharoshṭhī characters.

MONASTERY.

We shall now return to the lower court and make our way to the monastery on its eastern side. Just outside and to the left hand of the entrance is a small chapel containing a singularly beautiful group of stucco figures (Pl. XXVII). In the centre is seated the Buddha in the attitude of meditation (*dhyāna-mudrā*), with a standing Buddha to his right and left and two attendant figures behind. Of the latter, the one to the left carries the fly-whisk (*chaurī*), the other is the Vajrapāṇi, holding the thunderbolt in his left hand. On the central image are still many traces of the red and black paint and of the gold leaf with which it, and doubtless the other figures also, were once bedecked. A second group of figures to the left of this niche is unfortunately much damaged, but the realistic basket of fruits and flowers borne by one of the attendants is deserving of notice.

In plan and elevation, the monastery at Jauliāñ though slightly smaller, closely resembled the one at Mohṛā Morādu. There was the same open quadrangle with ranges of cells on its four sides; the same square depression in the middle of the quadrangle; the same small chamber, perhaps a bath-room, in the corner of the latter; the same verandah carried on wooden pillars; the same niches for images in front of the cells; the same kind of windows and lamp-niches inside them and the same stairway in one of the cells ascending to the upper storey. But in a few particulars this monastery helps to supplement the information acquired on the other site. Thus, some of the doorways of the cells are still intact, and we observe that they are much lower than might have been expected. It should be added, however, that the existing doorways belong to the later repair of the building, and it may have been that the original entrances of the Kushān period were higher. Again, on the northern side of the court, the cell immediately to the left of the stairway must have served as a shrine, since the remains of several burnt clay images, adorned with paint and gilding, were found inside it. The entrance of this particular cell is relieved by bands of floral designs roughly executed, like the images inside, in burnt clay; but in both cases the burning of the clay seems to have been caused by the general conflagra-

*JAULIAN: RELIEF IN NICHE.*

tion in which the whole monastery was involved during the fifth century A.D. Other evidences of this fire were also observable in the charred condition of floors and walls and in masses of charcoal and burnt timbers found in the cells and courtyard. That it took place during the fifth century is to be inferred both from the style of the sculptures, none of which can be referred to a later date than this, and from various minor antiquities found in the cells, among which was a burnt carnelian seal engraved with the words *Śrī Kulesvaradāsī* in Brāhmī characters of the Gupta age, and a birch bark manuscript also in Brāhmī of the same period. The latter, which is the first manuscript of the kind to be discovered in any excavation in India, is unfortunately sadly damaged by fire, but it is hoped that its partial decipherment may not prove impossible. Among the other antiquities found in the monastery were over 200 coins, many iron nails, hinges, and other implements, copper ornaments, terracottas and numerous potteries, including the several large store jars that are still to be seen in some of the cells.

## BHALLAṚ STŪPA.

Another large and important group of Buddhist monuments now being excavated is at the Bhallaṛ Stūpa, to which reference has been made on p. 60. They occupy a commanding position on the last spur of the Sarḍa hill, which bounds the Haro Valley on the north, and are situated at the side of the Havelian Railway, about 5 miles from Saraikala and half a mile north of the Haro river (Pl. XXVIII). The most convenient way to reach it is by means of a trolley, which can sometimes be obtained from the Sarai-kala Railway Station. The outward journey, which is mainly down hill, takes about 40 minutes, the return journey over an hour.

According to Hsüan Tsang,[1] the Bhallaṛ Stūpa was originally built by the Emperor Aśoka to commemorate the spot where Buddha in a previous existence[2] had made an offering of his head, but if ever Aśoka erected a monument here, no trace of it is now discoverable. The existing stūpa dates back no further than the third or fourth century of our era. Like the Kunāla stūpa on the opposite side of the valley, it stood on a lofty oblong base, ascended on its eastern side by a broad flight of steps. The body of the superstructure above this base, consisted, as usual, of a drum and dome surmounted by one or more umbrellas. The drum, which is strikingly high in proportion to the diameter of the monument, was divided into six or seven tiers, diminishing in size from the bottom upwards and decorated with rows of decadent Corinthian pilasters, friezes and dentil cornices. The northern half of the stūpa has entirely fallen and on this side the relic chamber, which was set near the top of the drum, is now exposed to view. In the court-

[1] *Cf.* Beal, *Buddhist Records of the Western World*, Vol. I, p. 138.

[2] *Cf. Div.* XXII, pp. 314—328. In that particular existence the Bodhisattva was Chandraprabha, and Taxila was the city of Bhadraśilā, over which he ruled. On the spot where the Bhallaṛ Stūpa now stands, there may once have been a Stūpa of a hero Chandraprabha, whose cult was subsequently absorbed into Buddhism.

PLATE XXVIII.

VIEW OF BHALLAR STUPA.

yard of the stūpa numerous chapels and other monuments are now being excavated, and the massive walls of a spacious monastery are just coming to light to the east of the courtyard; but it would be premature to speak of these until the digging is more advanced. It was in this monastery, says Hsüan Tsang, that Kumāralabdha, the founder of the Sautrāntika school, composed his treatises, and in the courtyard of the stūpa that a miracle took place not long before his time. A woman afflicted with leprosy came to worship at the stūpa, and, finding the court all covered with litter and dirty, she proceeded to cleanse it and to scatter flowers around the building. Thereupon her leprosy left her and her beauty was restored.

### Bhiṛ Mound.

In concluding this description of the ancient monuments of Taxila, it remains to mention a few finds made in the Bhiṛ Mound—the earliest of the three city sites. In this city digging operations have hitherto been limited to temporary trial trenches and pits, which have been sunk at various points, mainly towards the northern end of the site, and then filled in again. The remains thus disclosed comprise chambers of rough rubble masonry, potteries, terracotta figurines of primitive workmanship, coins and jewellery: all, so far as they can be dated, belonging to the Maurya epoch. The most noteworthy of these finds was a small treasure unearthed in the compound of the Archæological Bungalow. It consists of 160 punch-marked coins of debased silver, a very fine gold coin of Diodotus struck in the name of Antiochus II of Syria, a gold bangle, a gold pendant in the form of a tiger claw, a small gold reliquary and several other pieces of gold or silver jewellery, besides a large number of pearls, amethysts, garnets, corals and other stones. The gold pendant and the little reliquary are especially beautiful examples of the goldsmith's craft, the filigree design applied to their surface being remarkably delicate and refined. The coin of Antiochus and the local punch-marked coins point to the latter half of the 3rd century B.C. as the time when this jewellery was hidden in the ground, and the gold claw and the reliquary (Pl. XVI, *12*, *13* and *14*), which are more worn than the other pieces, are probably half a century or so earlier. By the side of the jewellery was found what appears to be a goldsmith's crucible with a few early Brāhmī characters stamped on its sides, and, in another chamber a narrow well filled with earthenware jars, all of which were turned upside down and empty. This well was excavated to a depth of some 18 feet, and about 50 vases were recovered. All these remains belong to the period of the Maurya occupation, when the city of Taxila was undoubtedly situated on the Bhiṛ Mound. As these remains, however, were quite near the surface, and as there is an artificial accumulation some 15 or 20 feet deep below them, there is every hope that remains of a much earlier period may be found in the lower strata.

# SHORT BIBLIOGRAPHY WITH ABBREVIATIONS


A. S. R. . . *Archæological Survey of India, Reports of the Director General* (Sir John Marshall), Parts I and II from 1902.

C. I. I. . . *Corpus Inscriptionum Indicarum.*

C. S. R. . . *Archæological Survey of India,* Reports of Sir Alex. Cunningham.

E. I. . . . *Epigraphia Indica.*

I. A. . . . *Indian Antiquary.*

J. A. . . . *Journal Asiatique.*

J. R. A. S. . . *Journal of the Royal Asiatic Society.*

BEAL, SAMUEL.—See Hiuen Thsang.

CUNNINGHAM, SIR ALEX.—*Coins of Alexander's successors in the East, the Greeks and Indo-Scythians, Part I.—The Greeks of Baktriana, Ariana and India*; London, 1869. *Coins of Ancient India from the earliest times to the seventh century A.D.*; London, 1891. *Coins of Mediæval India from the seventh century down to the Muhammadan conquests*; London, 1894. *Arch. Surv. Reports* (C. S. R.), Vols. I, II, V; Simla, Calcutta, 1871, 1875.

FA HIEN.—*A record of Buddhist kingdoms being an account of his travels in India and Ceylon (A.D. 399-414).* Trans. and annot. by James Legge; Oxford, 1886.

FERGUSSON, SIR J.—*History of Indian and Eastern Architecture*; 2nd ed., London, 1910.

FOUCHER, ALFRED.—*L'Art gréco-bouddhique du Gandhāra*; Paris, 1905; *Étude sur l'Iconographie bouddhique de l'Inde*; Paris, 1900, 1905.

GARDNER, PERCY.—*The Coins of Greek and Scythic kings of Bactria and India in the British Museum*; London, 1886.

GRÜNWEDEL, PROF. A.—*Buddhistische Kunst in Indien;* 2nd ed., Berlin, 1900. English trans. by A. C. Gibson and J. Burgess; London, 1901.

HIUEN THSANG (HSÜAN TSANG).—*Si-yu-ki, Buddhist records of the Western World.* Trans. by Samuel Beal, Vols. I-II; London, 1884.

*Jātaka or Stories of the Buddha's former births:* Engl. trans. ed. by E. B. Cowell; Vols. I-VII; Cambridge, 1895-1907.

MARSHALL, SIR JOHN.—*Annual Reports of the Director General of Archæology;* Calcutta, 1912-13, Pts. I and II; 1913-14, Pt. I; 1914-15, Pts. I and II; 1915-16, Pts. I and II.

MCCRINDLE, J. W.—*Ancient India as described by Megasthenes and Arrian* (From the Indian Antiquary); Calcutta, Bombay, London, 1877. *The Invasion of India by Alexander the Great as described by Arrian, Q. Curtius, Diodorus, Plutarch and Justin;* Westminister, 1896. *Ancient India as described in classical literature, being a collection of Greek and Latin texts relating to India extracted from Herodotus, Strabo, Diodorus Siculus, Pliny, Aelian, Philostratus, etc;* Westminister, 1901.

PHILOSTRATUS.—*The Life of Apollonius of Tyana,* with an English translation by F. C. Conybeare; New York, 1912.

RAPSON, E. J.—*Ancient India;* Cambridge, 1914.

SMITH, VINCENT.—*Catalogue of the Coins in the Indian Museum, Calcutta;* 1906. *Asoka, the Buddhist Emperor of India,* 2nd ed.; Oxford, 1909. *A history of fine Art in India and Ceylon;* Oxford, 1911. *Early History of India* [= *E. H. I.*] 3rd Ed.; Oxford, 1914.

WHITEHEAD, R. B.—*Catalogue of coins in the Panjab Museum, Lahore;* Oxford, 1914.

WATTERS, THOMAS.—*On Yuan Chwang's travels in India.* Vols. I and II; London, 1904-05.

WILSON, H. H.—*Ariana Antiqua;* London, 1841.

MAP OF
TAXILA
SIRSUKH
SIRKAP
BHIR MOUND

# GLOSSARY

**Acropolis.**—(*Gr.*=high city). The citadel or highest part of a Greek city, usually situated on an eminence commanding the rest of the town.

**Antæ.**—Pilasters terminating the side walls of a classic building.

**Apse.**—The termination of a building, circular, multangular or semi-circular in plan, with a domical or vaulted roof. The term was first applied to a Roman basilica.

**Architrave.**—The beam or lowest division of the entablature, which rests immediately on the column.

**Ashlar.**—Squared stonework in regular courses, in contradistinction to rubble work.

**Atlantes.**—Sculptured figures of men used in place of columns or pilasters, supporting or seeming to support a mass above them. Female figures used for the same purpose are known as Caryatides.

**Baluster.**—A small pillar supporting a handrail or coping, the whole being called a balustrade.

**Barbican.**—An outwork intended to defend the entrance to a castle or fortified town.

**Bodhisattva.**—See page 39, footnote 2.

**Cantharus.**—A two-handled drinking cup of Greek pattern.

**Cavetto.**—A small concave moulding.

**Coping.**—The capping of a wall or balustrade.

**Corbel.**—A block projecting from a wall to support a superincumbent weight.

**Cornice.**—In Greek architecture, the highest part of the entablature resting on the frieze; any moulded projection which crowns the part to which it is affixed. *Raking cornice*, a cornice inclining from the horizontal.

**Cyma.**—A moulding of which the profile is a double curve, concave and convex. *Cyma Recta*, in which the concave curve surmounts the convex; *cyma reversa*, in which the convex surmounts the concave.

**Dado.**—The lower part of a wall, when decorated separately.

**Dentil.**—Tooth-like ornamental blocks in Ionic and Corinthian cornices.

**Diaper.**—A small pattern repeated continuously over a wall surface. *Diaper masonry*, a distinctive kind of masonry illustrated on Plate V.

**En cabuchon.**—In the form of a carbuncle, *i.e.*, with a convex upper surface, in contradistinction to that of a garnet, which is facetted.

**Entablature.**—In classical architecture, that portion of a structure which is supported by the columns, and consists of the architrave, frieze and cornice.

**Entasis.**—A slight swelling in the shaft of a column.

**Fillet.**—A small flat moulding having the appearance of a narrow band, generally used to separate curvilinear mouldings.

**Frieze.**—That part of the entablature which is between the architrave and cornice, usually enriched with figures or other ornaments.

**Frontality.**—A term applied to archaic statues, which are so rigidly and formally fashioned, that an imaginary plane drawn through the top of the head, nose, backbone, breastbone and navel, divides the figure into two perfectly symmetrical halves.

**Glyptic.**—Pertaining to the art of engraving.

**Intaglio.**—An engraved figure sunk into the face of a gem: the reverse of a cameo, which is in relief.

**Jātaka, The.**—A Pali work containing 550 stories about the previous births of Gautama Buddha, who, according to the Buddhist belief, had been born in all created forms, as man, god and animal, before he appeared on earth as the son of Śuddhodana.

KAÑJŪR.—The local name of a soft limestone.

KHAROSHṬHĪ.—A script derived from Aramaic; it was in vogue in the North-West of India between B.C. 300 and 400 A.D.

MAHĀBHĀRATA.—The great Sanskrit Epic of India, the theme of which is the war between the sons of Kuru and the sons of Pandu. It consists of 18 books and is commonly attributed to the sage Vyāsa.

NANDIPADA.—'Footprint of Nandi,' a device frequently found on ancient coins and supposed to represent the footprint of a bull.

OGEE.—A moulding or arch, of which the curve resembles the cyma reversa (q.v.).

PEDIMENT.—The triangular termination of the roof of a classic temple; in Gothic architecture called the "gable."

PERIPTERAL.—An edifice surrounded by a range of columns.

PERISTYLE.—A range of columns surrounding a court or temple.

PILASTER.—A square pillar projecting from a wall.

PRADAKSHIṆA.—A ceremonial act performed by walking round a stūpa or other sacred edifice from left to right.

PRAKRIT.—The vernacular dialect of ancient India. The various forms of Prakrit are closely allied to literary Sanskrit.

PYXIS.—A Greek jewel box.

REPOUSSÉ.—A style of ornamentation in metal, raised in relief by hammering from behind.

RIDGE-ROOF.—A raised or peaked roof.

ROCOCO.—A debased variety of ornament, in which the decorative devices lack good taste and meaning.

SATĪ.—(*Skr.*). A widow who immolates herself on the funeral pyre of her husband.

SATRAP.—(*Kshatrapa*) Viceroy or Governor of a province. The title was originally a Persian one.

SCOTIA.—A concave moulding used principally in the bases of columns and walls.

SOFFIT.—The underside of any architectural member.

STEATITE.—A stone commonly known as soap-stone.

STŪPA.—See p. 35, footnote 1.

TORAṆA.—A gateway of Indian design. See p. 29, footnote 1.

TORUS.—A convex moulding used principally in the bases of columns.

TRIRATNA.—(*Skr.*) 'Three jewels.' A trident-like device used to symbolise the trinity of Buddhism. See p. 41, footnote 1.

UNIFACIAL.—A term used of archaic statuary in the round which is conceived by the sculptor in one aspect only, in contradistinction to the plurifacial statuary of developed art, which is conceived simultaneously in all its aspects, *i.e.*, in its three dimensions.

USHṆĪSHA.—See p. 44, footnote 1.

VAJRAPĀṆI.—(*Skr.*) 'Bearer of the thunderbolt.' An attendant on the Buddha, whose identity is uncertain.

VISHṆU PURĀṆA.—One of the 18 Purāṇas, which deal with creation, with the genealogies of gods and patriarchs and with the dynasties of kings. The dynastic history given in the *Vishṇu Puraṇa* extends to the rise of the Imperial Guptas in the 4th century A.D.

VOLUTE.—The scroll or spiral in Ionic and Corinthian capitals.

CALCUTTA: PRINTED BY SUPDT. GOVT. PRINTING, INDIA, 8, HASTINGS STREET.